I0013336

CHRIS DEVON

C# unity Programming For Beginners

Copyright © 2024 by Chris Devon

All rights reserved. No part of this publication may be reproduced, stored or transmitted in any form or by any means, electronic, mechanical, photocopying, recording, scanning, or otherwise without written permission from the publisher. It is illegal to copy this book, post it to a website, or distribute it by any other means without permission.

First edition

This book was professionally typeset on Reedsy.
Find out more at reedsy.com

Contents

Introduction: Getting Started with C# and Unity

Why Choose Unity and C# for Game Development?
When beginning a journey into game development, two essential decisions are choosing a suitable game engine and programming language. Unity, paired with C#, stands out as a versatile, approachable, and powerful combination for beginners and professionals alike. The synergy between Unity's extensive toolset and C#'s efficient and beginner-friendly syntax offers a gateway into creating engaging, dynamic games across various platforms. This section delves into the unique qualities of Unity and C# and the reasons they have become staples for developers around the world.

1. Unity: A Comprehensive Game Development Platform

Unity is one of the most widely used game development engines globally. It provides a complete suite of tools that support creating both 2D and 3D games, along with augmented reality (AR) and virtual reality (VR) experiences. The engine's flexibility and its community-driven development make it an ideal starting point for both indie developers and large studios.

- **Cross-Platform Capability**: Unity allows developers to build games for a wide array of platforms, including PC, Mac, iOS, Android, PlayStation, Xbox, and WebGL. This cross-platform compatibility ensures that you can design a game and deploy it to multiple devices, reaching a larger audience without significantly altering the code. For indie developers and small studios, this versatility is invaluable as it maximizes the potential player base with minimal additional effort.

- **Intuitive Interface and Workflow**: One of Unity's major strengths lies in its user-friendly interface. Designed with both beginners and experienced developers in mind, Unity's interface is organized, intuitive, and highly customizable. For new users, Unity offers an easy learning curve with drag-and-drop components and an asset-based design approach, reducing the amount of coding required for certain aspects. For more experienced developers, Unity's flexible architecture allows fine-tuned control over every aspect of the game.

- **Real-Time Rendering and Visual Fidelity**: Unity's rendering engine provides impressive visual fidelity, and with tools like the Unity Shader Graph, you can create complex visual effects without deep knowledge of graphics programming. Unity's support for HDRP (High-Definition Render Pipeline) and URP (Universal Render Pipeline) allows developers to balance visual quality with performance for different devices, making Unity suitable for both high-end PC games and mobile games that prioritize performance.

- **Asset Store and Community**: Unity boasts one of the most extensive asset stores, filled with models, textures, animations, scripts, and tools created by other developers. This asset library can speed up the development process by providing ready-made elements that you can customize, freeing up time to focus on unique game mechanics and design. Additionally, Unity's large user community contributes to forums, tutorials, and documentation, offering invaluable resources for troubleshooting and skill development.

2. The Role of C# in Unity Development

C# is the primary scripting language for Unity, and its integration into the engine is one of the factors that makes Unity such an effective and flexible development tool. Known for its readability, structured syntax, and powerful libraries, C# is an ideal language for beginners and experts alike in game development.

- **Beginner-Friendly Syntax**: C# offers a balance between simplicity and depth. Unlike languages that require a steep learning curve, C#'s syntax is straightforward and clean, making it approachable for new programmers. Concepts such as variables, loops, and conditional statements in C# are intuitively structured, and the language's consistency helps beginners learn faster.
- **Object-Oriented Programming (OOP) Principles**: C# is a fully object-oriented language, which aligns perfectly with Unity's component-based architecture. Object-oriented programming is a paradigm that organizes code into objects, which allows for modular, reusable, and manageable code. In Unity, every element in a game, from the player to individual obstacles, is represented as a GameObject, which can contain various components, such as physics properties and scripts. Understanding how to work with C# and Unity's object-oriented design is a powerful advantage, as it promotes good coding practices and supports scalability for larger, more complex games.
- **Rich Standard Library and Frameworks**: C# comes with a vast standard library, covering everything from data management to networking and file manipulation. Unity-specific frameworks, such as the UnityEngine namespace, provide classes for handling game physics, input, UI elements, audio, and graphics. With C#, you have access to these resources, making it easier to implement a wide range of functionality without relying heavily on third-party plugins or extensive coding.
- **Strong Typing and Compile-Time Checking**: Unlike dynamically-typed languages, C# is statically-typed, meaning that data types must be defined upfront. This reduces errors and makes code more predictable and robust. Unity's Visual Studio integration supports C# debugging, allowing you to catch syntax errors and runtime issues early in the development process. This feature alone can save significant time by reducing the number of bugs and improving the stability of your game.

3. Unity and C# Synergy: A Seamless Workflow

Unity's architecture is designed to work harmoniously with C#, allowing you to leverage both to their full potential.

- **Component-Based Design in Unity**: Unity's GameObject-Component system is designed to facilitate modular design, which aligns naturally with C#'s OOP structure. Every game element in Unity can be thought of as a GameObject, to which components, such as scripts, physics, and UI elements, are attached. This modular approach allows developers to build complex behaviors by combining and reusing components, streamlining the development process. C# scripts can be written for individual components, enabling each to handle specific functions, making it easier to manage and organize code as a game grows in complexity.

- **Event-Driven Programming**: Unity's event-driven approach, coupled with C#'s delegate and event system, provides a powerful way to manage interactions in games. For example, when a player character collides with an object, Unity can trigger an event (like a collision detection) that activates a C# script to respond to that interaction. This event-driven model allows for responsive and dynamic gameplay mechanics that keep players engaged and adds complexity to game logic without overcomplicating code.

- **Integrated Development Environment (IDE) Support**: Unity developers benefit from seamless integration with Visual Studio, the official IDE for C# development. Visual Studio's robust set of tools, including IntelliSense (code suggestion), debugging capabilities, and syntax highlighting, enhance the development experience. For beginners, Visual Studio's intelligent suggestions and error-checking make it easier to learn and correct mistakes in real-time, while experienced developers gain access to tools for writing efficient, scalable code.

4. Unity and C# for Prototyping and Iteration

One of Unity's most celebrated features is its rapid prototyping capabilities, which allow developers to quickly create, test, and refine ideas. For beginners, this rapid iteration is invaluable for learning through experimentation and seeing immediate results from coding changes.

- **Real-Time Testing**: Unity's Play Mode lets developers test their game directly in the editor, enabling rapid feedback on game mechanics, physics interactions, and player controls. With C#, developers can make adjustments to scripts, recompile, and immediately see the impact on gameplay, greatly reducing downtime.
- **Efficient Asset and Code Management**: Unity's Prefab system allows for the creation of reusable assets—complete with attached C# scripts and components—that can be updated across the entire game from a single source. This capability is highly beneficial for prototyping as it allows developers to create and modify game objects with minimal rework.
- **Support for Agile Development Practices**: Unity's ease of use and C#'s flexibility align with agile development practices, enabling incremental builds and rapid iteration. For developers looking to test different game mechanics, themes, or visual elements, Unity and C# provide a supportive environment that promotes quick testing, refinement, and feedback integration.

5. Career and Community Benefits of Unity and C# Skills

Unity and C# are in high demand across the game development industry, with a strong presence in both indie and AAA studios. Proficiency in Unity and C# is a valuable asset for aspiring game developers, and mastering these tools opens doors to a wide range of career opportunities.

- **Industry Standard**: Unity is used by numerous companies and independent developers worldwide, making it a skill recognized by potential employers and project collaborators. Unity's flexibility allows it to be used in non-gaming applications as well, including simulations, architectural visualization, and VR training programs, which broadens the career scope for Unity developers.

- **Expansive and Supportive Community**: The Unity developer community is one of the largest and most active in the game industry, with countless forums, tutorials, online courses, and documentation. This community support provides valuable resources for troubleshooting, skill-building, and project feedback. For new developers, access to a wealth of free resources and guidance significantly enhances learning and lowers the barrier to entry.
- **Ecosystem of Learning Resources**: Unity and C# are popular choices for learning institutions and online platforms, meaning that beginners have access to a rich ecosystem of learning materials, from documentation and tutorials to online courses and certifications. For beginners, these resources accelerate the learning process, providing structured paths to proficiency.

The Best Choice for Aspiring Game Developers

The combination of Unity and C# offers an unparalleled entry point into game development, blending accessible tools with powerful functionality that allows you to develop skills as a programmer and designer. Unity's intuitive interface, robust asset pipeline, and C#'s logical structure create a cohesive, adaptable platform that empowers developers to turn their game ideas into reality. By choosing Unity and C#, beginners and experienced developers alike gain access to a streamlined development environment where creativity and technical skills can flourish, making it one of the most compelling choices in the game development industry today.

Overview of Unity's Capabilities: 2D, 3D, AR, and VR

Unity stands out in the game development industry for its versatility and adaptability. Its capabilities extend far beyond the standard 2D and 3D game creation; the engine also supports advanced and emerging fields like augmented reality (AR) and virtual reality (VR). This expansive toolkit makes Unity an attractive option for developers looking to create across a variety of experiences and platforms. Let's explore how Unity's 2D, 3D, AR, and VR capabilities equip developers to bring diverse and immersive projects to life.

1. 2D Game Development: A Robust Toolkit for Side-Scrolling, Puzzle, and Mobile Games

Unity's 2D toolset is comprehensive, offering everything developers need to create side-scrolling platformers, puzzle games, and other 2D experiences. Although Unity initially rose to fame with its 3D capabilities, its 2D tools have matured significantly, making it one of the top choices for developers looking to create visually rich and performance-optimized 2D games.

- **Sprite Management and Animation**: Unity's sprite management system makes it easy to import and organize 2D images (sprites) that form the basis of a 2D game. Unity's built-in Sprite Editor allows developers to slice sprite sheets into individual sprites, enabling smooth animation for character movements and interactions. The Animator tool, used in conjunction with sprites, allows for complex animations and transitions without extensive code, which is particularly useful for creating responsive and visually engaging character animations.
- **Tilemaps and Level Design**: Unity's Tilemap system simplifies the process of building game levels. With Tilemaps, developers can design grid-based levels quickly, laying down walls, floors, and other environmental elements without manually placing each tile. This approach not only speeds up the design process but also ensures consistent scaling and alignment. Unity's Tile Palette tool further enhances efficiency by allowing developers to paint entire scenes or levels with predefined tiles, making it ideal for games with large, grid-based maps, like platformers or strategy games.
- **2D Physics and Collisions**: Unity's 2D physics engine is optimized for side-scrollers and top-down games, providing realistic physics

simulations with minimal setup. Components like Rigidbody2D and Collider2D enable developers to create gravity, friction, collisions, and bounce effects, bringing realism to gameplay. The physics system is intuitive and straightforward, allowing even beginners to create dynamic interactions, such as a character bouncing off platforms or collecting items.

- **User-Friendly UI for Mobile and 2D Games**: Unity's UI system is flexible enough to cater to both 2D and 3D applications. For 2D games, Unity's Canvas system allows developers to position UI elements—such as buttons, health bars, and score counters—relative to the screen space, ensuring they scale and align properly across different devices. This feature is particularly useful for mobile games, where consistent UI layout across various screen sizes is essential.

2. 3D Game Development: Immersive Environments and Realistic Gameplay

Unity's origins lie in 3D game development, and over the years, it has become one of the most powerful engines for creating 3D games. Its tools enable developers to build everything from simple mobile 3D games to complex, high-fidelity simulations for PC and console.

- **Flexible 3D Asset Pipeline**: Unity supports a wide range of 3D file formats, including FBX, OBJ, and DAE, making it easy to import models created in external 3D modeling software like Blender, Maya, or 3ds Max. This compatibility allows for seamless integration of complex models into Unity, enabling developers to create detailed characters, environments, and props with ease.
- **Lighting and Rendering Systems**: Unity's rendering engine includes powerful lighting options that add depth and realism to 3D games. With the High-Definition Render Pipeline (HDRP) and Universal Render Pipeline (URP), developers can control lighting effects such as real-time shadows, reflections, and global illumination. HDRP is ideal for high-end games on PC and console, providing cinematic visual quality,

while URP is optimized for mobile devices, balancing performance with graphical fidelity.

- **Physics and Rigidbodies for Realistic Interactions**: Unity's 3D physics engine supports Rigidbody and Collider components, which enable developers to simulate physical interactions in a realistic manner. These components allow for complex behaviors, like gravity, momentum, and collision detection, enabling games to include elements such as destructible environments, character movement, and object interactions. With customizable physics settings, Unity makes it possible to create anything from highly realistic simulations to arcade-style physics with exaggerated behaviors.

- **Cameras and Cinematics**: Unity provides extensive camera tools for setting up and controlling in-game perspectives. The Cinemachine feature, in particular, allows developers to create smooth camera transitions, dynamic framing, and complex camera behaviors without needing extensive programming. Cinemachine is essential for creating cinematic cutscenes, providing a professional polish to any 3D game by enabling camera paths, transitions, and automated focus adjustments that respond to player actions or specific game events.

3. Augmented Reality (AR): Bridging Digital and Physical Worlds

Unity is one of the leading platforms for AR development, providing developers with tools to create experiences that overlay digital elements onto the real world. Through partnerships with ARKit (Apple) and ARCore (Google), Unity supports AR experiences across iOS and Android devices, enabling developers to reach a broad audience.

- **AR Foundation**: Unity's AR Foundation framework unifies ARKit and ARCore, allowing developers to build a single AR application that runs on both iOS and Android with minimal platform-specific code. AR Foundation provides a standardized API for common AR features such as plane detection, image tracking, face tracking, and 3D object placement.

9

- **Plane and Image Recognition**: AR games and applications rely on detecting real-world surfaces, such as floors or tables, where digital objects can be placed. Unity's AR Foundation enables plane detection, allowing developers to anchor digital elements to flat surfaces in the physical world. Additionally, image recognition allows Unity apps to recognize and interact with specific images in the real world, opening up possibilities for interactive experiences based on printed materials or signs.

- **Object Placement and Interaction**: Unity's support for 3D object placement and interaction is ideal for creating AR applications that allow users to visualize products, play AR-based games, or interact with educational content. With tools for touch and gesture input, developers can enable users to move, rotate, and scale virtual objects as they appear in the real world, creating immersive and engaging experiences.

- **Real-World Applications Beyond Gaming**: Unity's AR capabilities have significant potential beyond gaming. In retail, AR applications can help customers visualize products in their home environments; in education, AR can enhance learning by adding interactive elements to physical objects. Unity's versatility allows developers to explore various applications of AR technology, from training simulations to interactive media, making it a valuable tool for AR experiences across multiple sectors.

4. Virtual Reality (VR): Fully Immersive Experiences

Unity's VR capabilities allow developers to create immersive worlds where players can explore and interact in a 3D space. Unity supports a range of VR headsets, including Oculus, HTC Vive, and PlayStation VR, making it accessible for both high-end and consumer VR development.

- **VR Ready Rendering and Optimization**: VR requires optimized rendering to ensure smooth and immersive experiences at high frame rates. Unity's URP and XR Interaction Toolkit provide tools specifically tailored for VR optimization, focusing on performance without compromising visual quality. The XR Interaction Toolkit streamlines the development of VR applications by offering a set of pre-built tools for interacting with virtual objects.

- **Intuitive Interaction Design with VR Controllers**: Unity supports VR controllers that allow users to interact with virtual environments naturally. Unity's XR Interaction Toolkit includes tools for managing input from VR controllers, simplifying the setup of gestures, grips, and object manipulation. This toolkit also includes teleportation features, which let users move within a VR space without inducing motion sickness, improving comfort for extended use.

- **Spatial Audio and Environmental Immersion**: Audio is a vital component of VR immersion. Unity's spatial audio capabilities allow developers to create realistic soundscapes where audio cues come from specific directions, enhancing the sense of presence. By adjusting audio to respond to player position and movement, Unity enables a more immersive experience, where sounds help guide players through the virtual environment.

- **Expanding VR Beyond Games**: Unity's VR capabilities are used in fields beyond gaming, including medical training, real estate tours, and educational simulations. In these applications, VR enables hands-on learning in a risk-free environment, improving retention and engagement. Unity's versatility in VR development means that developers can explore immersive experiences across various industries, utilizing the same tools that power VR games to create impactful training and educational applications.

5. Unity's Versatility Across Platforms and Mediums

One of Unity's greatest strengths is its versatility across various development mediums and platforms. Whether creating a mobile 2D game, a PC-based 3D RPG, or a VR educational tool, Unity offers tools and support for developers to bring their vision to life on almost any device. This multi-platform adaptability allows Unity developers to innovate across various fields and reach diverse audiences.

Unity's support for 2D, 3D, AR, and VR means that it caters to a wide spectrum of development needs, enabling beginners and seasoned professionals alike to explore different genres and interactive mediums. By mastering Unity's capabilities, developers can expand their skill set and adapt to the demands of a constantly evolving technology landscape, making Unity an invaluable asset for any aspiring game developer.

Choosing Unity for Limitless Possibilities

Unity's capabilities in 2D, 3D, AR, and VR make it a comprehensive and versatile development engine, empowering developers to create a vast range of interactive experiences. This adaptability enables developers to target various platforms and mediums without needing to switch between engines or learn new toolsets. By leveraging Unity's robust ecosystem, developers can not only create engaging games but also explore emerging fields like AR and VR, placing themselves at the forefront of digital innovation. Unity's flexibility and power make it the ideal engine for developers eager to experiment, iterate, and bring unique ideas to life.

Installing Unity and Setting Up Your Environment

Setting up Unity and preparing your development environment is an essential first step toward game creation. This process involves installing the Unity Hub, downloading the correct version of Unity, and configuring your settings to optimize productivity. By following this guide, you'll be well-prepared to begin developing games, with all the necessary tools organized and ready for efficient workflow.

1. Downloading Unity Hub: A Centralized Management Tool

Unity Hub is a management application that allows you to install and manage multiple versions of Unity, organize your projects, and access essential resources like tutorials and the Unity Asset Store. Unity Hub is highly recommended as it streamlines the setup process and helps you stay organized, particularly when working with multiple projects or Unity versions.

- **Step-by-Step Installation**:

Visit the Unity Website: Go to unity.com and navigate to the download section.

Download Unity Hub: Select and download the Unity Hub installer compatible with your operating system (Windows, macOS, or Linux).

Install Unity Hub: Run the installer and follow the prompts to complete the installation.

- **Unity Hub Interface Overview**:
- **Projects Tab**: This tab lists all your current projects, allowing you to organize, open, or create new ones.
- **Learn Tab**: Unity provides access to tutorials, sample projects, and documentation here—ideal for beginners.
- **Installs Tab**: Here, you can manage the Unity versions installed on your computer, allowing you to add, remove, or update them as needed.
- **Community and Preferences**: Access Unity forums and manage your personal settings, including project paths and editor preferences, to personalize your experience.

2. **Installing Unity Through Unity Hub**

Unity regularly releases updates and different versions to accommodate various features, fixes, and optimizations. For new projects, the latest stable release is generally recommended, as it includes the newest features and the latest improvements.

- **Adding a Unity Version**:

Open Unity Hub and Go to the Installs Tab: This is where you manage all Unity versions on your system.

Add a New Version: Click "Add" and select the latest official release (indicated with a blue "Recommended" label). Unity Hub also offers pre-release and LTS (Long Term Support) versions. LTS versions are ideal for projects that prioritize stability over the latest features.

Choose Modules to Install: During installation, Unity offers additional modules, such as platform build supports (iOS, Android, WebGL) and development tools like Visual Studio. Select these based on your needs, but keep in mind that mobile and WebGL support are beneficial if you're planning to release on those platforms.

Download and Install: Once you've selected your desired modules, click "Install." Unity Hub will download and set up the chosen Unity version.

3. Setting Up Visual Studio: Your Primary Coding Environment

Unity integrates closely with Visual Studio (VS), an integrated development environment (IDE) that simplifies coding in C# with features like syntax highlighting, debugging, and error-checking. Visual Studio is typically offered as an optional download during Unity installation, but you can also install it separately.

- **Downloading and Configuring Visual Studio**:
- If Visual Studio wasn't installed during Unity setup, you can download it from the Visual Studio website. Select the Community edition, which is free for individual use and provides all necessary features.
- During installation, ensure you select the **.NET desktop development** and **Game development with Unity** workloads, as these provide the necessary tools for working in Unity.
- **Integrating Visual Studio with Unity**:
- Unity should automatically detect Visual Studio if it's installed. If not, you can link it manually by going to **Edit > Preferences > External Tools** in Unity and selecting Visual Studio as the External Script Editor.
- This integration allows you to open Unity scripts directly in Visual Studio by double-clicking on them in Unity's Project window, provid-

ing a smooth transition between the Unity Editor and your coding environment.

4. Creating Your First Project in Unity

After installing Unity and setting up Visual Studio, you're ready to create your first Unity project. Unity Hub simplifies this process, allowing you to configure project settings and choose templates that match your game's requirements.

- **Steps to Create a New Project**:

Open Unity Hub and Click 'New Project': This option is located on the Projects tab.

Select a Template: Unity offers several templates tailored to different types of projects:

- **3D Core**: Ideal for general 3D projects, featuring standard 3D graphics and physics tools.
- **2D Core**: Optimized for 2D games, with default settings for 2D sprite management, physics, and lighting.
- **High Definition RP (HDRP)**: Recommended for high-fidelity, graphically intensive projects intended for powerful platforms like PC or console.
- **Universal RP (URP)**: Designed for a balance between performance and quality, suitable for cross-platform projects, including mobile and desktop.
- **AR and VR Templates**: Pre-configured for augmented and virtual reality projects, offering tools for head tracking, interaction, and rendering optimizations.

Name Your Project and Choose a Location: Give your project a meaningful name and choose a directory on your computer to save it. Unity will generate a project folder in this location, where all assets and settings are stored.

Create Project: Once your settings are configured, click "Create." Unity will open the project in the Editor, displaying a blank canvas ready for development.

5. Exploring the Unity Editor: Key Panels and Tools

When you first open Unity, the Editor interface may seem overwhelming, but understanding its core panels will help you navigate and use it effectively. The Editor's layout is designed to be flexible, allowing you to rearrange and customize panels based on your preferences.

- **Scene View and Game View**:
- **Scene View**: This is your main workspace, where you create and position GameObjects, adjust lighting, and design your game's environment. It provides a 3D (or 2D) visualization of your game, showing objects and allowing direct manipulation.
- **Game View**: A preview of how your game will appear to players when it runs. This view simulates the in-game camera's perspective and is essential for testing gameplay elements as you develop.
- **Hierarchy Panel**: The Hierarchy panel displays all GameObjects in the current scene, organized in a tree structure. Objects can be parented to each other, creating hierarchies that help manage complex scenes. For instance, you might group all elements of a player character (e.g., body, head, arms) under a single parent GameObject.
- **Inspector Panel**: The Inspector displays the properties and components of the currently selected GameObject. Here, you can adjust settings like position, rotation, scale, and specific component settings (such as Rigidbody properties for physics objects or Audio Source properties for sound).
- **Project Panel**: This panel shows all the assets and resources used in your project, organized in a folder structure. It's essentially your project's file explorer, allowing you to import, organize, and manage textures, scripts, prefabs, and other resources.

- **Console**: The Console is used for debugging and displays error messages, warnings, and custom log messages. This is where Unity outputs any errors or issues with scripts, providing essential information for troubleshooting.

6. Configuring Project Settings for Performance and Compatibility
Project Settings allow you to fine-tune how Unity runs, affecting aspects like performance, input, and graphics quality. Configuring these settings early on can help optimize your game and ensure it runs smoothly across different devices.

- **Quality Settings**: Located in **Edit > Project Settings > Quality**, these settings let you define various quality levels (e.g., Low, Medium, High) for your game. Quality settings control visual fidelity and performance trade-offs, which is crucial when developing for multiple platforms.
- **Input Settings**: Unity's default Input Manager supports handling inputs like keyboard, mouse, touch, and controllers. Customize input settings in **Edit > Project Settings > Input Manager** to map control schemes that fit your game design, particularly if you plan to support multiple input devices.
- **Player Settings**: Located under **Edit > Project Settings > Player**, this section allows you to configure your game's build settings, including resolution, icon, and splash screen. Here, you can also enable or disable platform-specific settings, such as optimization for iOS or Android.
- **Scripting Runtime and API Compatibility**: Found in **Edit > Project Settings > Player > Other Settings**, Unity allows you to select the .NET runtime version and API compatibility. The default setting usually works well for most projects, but certain third-party libraries may require changes to compatibility settings.

7. Saving and Backing Up Your Project
Saving your project regularly and maintaining backups is essential, especially as your project grows in complexity. Unity's file structure makes

it easy to create backups, but it's important to follow best practices to avoid data loss.

- **Saving Your Scene**: In Unity, "saving" doesn't automatically save all elements of your project. You need to save each scene individually by going to **File > Save Scene** or **File > Save Scene As**. Scenes are the primary units of work in Unity, so be diligent about saving whenever you make changes.
- **Creating Project Backups**: To create a backup of your project, copy the entire project folder to a safe location. Cloud storage services like Google Drive, Dropbox, or GitHub (using Git for version control) are useful for backing up your project and enabling version tracking. This is especially valuable when collaborating with others or working on large projects.
- **Version Control with Git**: For more robust backup and version tracking, consider using Git with a service like GitHub or GitLab. Unity projects are compatible with Git, allowing you to save incremental changes, branch out for new features, and revert to previous versions if needed.

8. Unity's Documentation and Community Resources

Unity's extensive documentation and active developer community are invaluable resources, especially for beginners. The documentation covers every Unity feature, offering examples and explanations that can help you understand each tool and component in depth.

- **Unity Documentation**: Accessible directly from Unity's **Help** menu, this documentation provides detailed explanations of Unity's components, APIs, and workflows. It's an excellent resource when you need clarification on a specific feature.
- **Unity Forums and Answers**: The Unity forums and Answers platform are filled with discussions, tips, and solutions contributed by Unity developers. These communities are supportive and collaborative,

making it easier to solve issues and learn from experienced developers.

- **Unity Learn and Tutorials**: Unity Learn offers structured tutorials and learning paths for various aspects of game development. These courses range from beginner basics to advanced techniques and are ideal for building foundational skills.

A Fully Prepared Development Environment

By following these steps, you'll have Unity, Visual Studio, and the essential tools configured and ready for game development. This initial setup ensures that you have an organized workspace and the resources needed to develop and test games efficiently. With your environment set up, you're ready to start building your first Unity project and dive deeper into the world of game development.

Navigating the Unity Interface: Key Panels and Tools

The Unity interface is designed to streamline the game development process, providing intuitive tools and panels that allow developers to create, test, and refine their projects. Familiarizing yourself with Unity's core panels and understanding how each one functions will enhance your workflow and make development smoother and more efficient. This section explores the Unity interface, breaking down each of the key panels and tools that you'll use regularly in game creation.

1. Scene View and Game View: Your Workspace and Preview

The Scene View and Game View are two of Unity's primary panels, each serving distinct but complementary roles in the development process.

- **Scene View**: This is your main workspace where you'll build, organize, and visualize your game environment. The Scene View allows you to freely move the camera, view your GameObjects from any angle, and manipulate them directly within the 2D or 3D space. Whether you're arranging characters, placing objects, or setting up your lighting, the Scene View provides a flexible environment for design.

- **Navigation**: You can navigate the Scene View using the mouse and keyboard shortcuts. For example, right-clicking and dragging moves the camera, while the scroll wheel zooms in and out. Pressing the "F" key focuses on a selected GameObject, centering it within the view.
- **Tools for Manipulation**: Unity offers various manipulation tools— Move, Rotate, Scale, and Rect Transform. These tools, located at the top of the Scene View, allow you to adjust the position, orientation, and size of GameObjects. Each tool is represented by a unique icon, making it easy to switch between them as needed.
- **Game View**: While Scene View is a free-form editor, Game View is a preview of how your game will appear to players. This view renders the scene from the perspective of your main camera, displaying the game as if it were running on a device. The Game View is essential for testing gameplay, as it lets you see exactly how players will experience the environment, controls, and UI.
- **Aspect Ratios and Resolutions**: Unity's Game View offers settings to test different aspect ratios and resolutions, ensuring that your game looks good on various devices. You can select predefined ratios like 16:9 or 4:3, or set custom resolutions to match specific device requirements.
- **Maximize on Play**: Selecting this option expands the Game View to fill the entire editor window when you enter Play Mode, allowing you to get a full-screen preview of your game.

2. Hierarchy Panel: Managing GameObjects and Scene Organization

The Hierarchy panel displays every GameObject within the current scene, organized in a hierarchical tree structure. Each object in the scene, from characters and terrain to lights and cameras, is listed in this panel.

- **Parent-Child Relationships**: Unity's Hierarchy uses a parent-child structure that enables you to group related GameObjects together. For example, if you have a player character with several components (body, head, arms), you can group these as children under a single parent GameObject. Moving or scaling the parent GameObject will also affect its children, allowing you to manage complex scenes with ease.

- **Reordering and Grouping**: You can drag GameObjects within the Hierarchy to reorder them or create nested hierarchies. Grouping objects together under empty GameObjects (also called "containers") is a common practice, as it keeps the Hierarchy organized and makes large scenes easier to navigate.
- **Enabling and Disabling Objects**: By toggling the checkbox next to each GameObject's name in the Hierarchy, you can enable or disable it. Disabling a GameObject will remove it from the Game View but keep it available in the Scene View, which is useful for testing different configurations or hiding elements temporarily.

3. Inspector Panel: Adjusting Properties and Components

The Inspector panel provides detailed information and customization options for the selected GameObject. Whenever you click on an object in the Scene or Hierarchy, the Inspector displays its properties and components.

- **Transform Component**: Every GameObject has a Transform component that defines its position, rotation, and scale. This component is fundamental, as it determines where the object is located in the scene and how it's oriented.
- **Adding Components**: Unity's component-based architecture allows you to add behavior and functionality to GameObjects by attaching components. The Add Component button in the Inspector lets you attach scripts, physics components (like Rigidbody or Colliders), UI elements, and more to an object. Each component adds a set of properties that can be adjusted directly in the Inspector.
- **Editing Properties**: You can modify each component's properties in the Inspector by adjusting values, checking boxes, and selecting options from dropdown menus. These changes affect the GameObject in real-time, allowing you to see the impact of adjustments immediately in the

Scene and Game Views.

4. Project Panel: Organizing Assets and Resources

The Project panel acts as a file explorer for all assets in your project, including textures, scripts, models, prefabs, audio, and more. It mirrors the folder structure on your computer, helping you manage the files that Unity will include in your game build.

- **Folder Organization**: It's a good practice to create folders for different asset types (e.g., Textures, Scripts, Prefabs, Audio) to keep the Project panel organized. Proper organization not only makes assets easier to find but also enhances workflow efficiency, especially in large projects.
- **Asset Importing**: You can import assets into Unity by dragging them from your file explorer directly into the Project panel. Unity automatically converts and optimizes files for use within the engine, making it simple to add new resources as needed.
- **Creating Prefabs**: Prefabs are reusable, customizable GameObjects that you can store in the Project panel and instantiate in your scenes. For instance, if you create a custom enemy GameObject with specific components and properties, you can turn it into a prefab to reuse it across multiple levels or scenes without recreating it from scratch.

5. Console Panel: Debugging and Error Checking

The Console panel is a vital tool for debugging and tracking issues within your project. It displays error messages, warnings, and logs generated by your scripts, allowing you to identify and fix problems as you develop.

- **Log Messages**: The Console provides feedback from your scripts through Debug.Log, Debug.Warning, and Debug.Error statements, which you can insert into your code. This is useful for tracking the flow of operations, checking variable values, and identifying issues as they occur.
- **Error Tracking**: When there's an error in your code, the Console

highlights it with a red message. Clicking on the error message opens the corresponding script in Visual Studio, allowing you to jump directly to the line of code that caused the issue.

- **Clearing and Filtering Logs**: Unity allows you to filter logs by type (Log, Warning, Error) to view specific messages. You can also clear the Console to remove old messages and focus on current issues, keeping your workspace uncluttered.

6. Toolbar: Essential Tools and Play Controls

The Toolbar at the top of Unity's interface contains essential controls for running, pausing, and stopping the game, as well as icons for accessing transformation tools.

- **Play Mode Controls**: The Play, Pause, and Step buttons control Play Mode, which allows you to test your game directly within the Unity Editor. Play Mode runs the game in real-time, simulating how it will behave upon release. While in Play Mode, any changes made to GameObjects are temporary and revert when exiting, helping you experiment without permanently altering your scene.
- **Transform Tools**: The Move, Rotate, and Scale tools are icons that allow you to adjust GameObjects in the Scene View. Unity also offers shortcuts (W for Move, E for Rotate, and R for Scale) to switch between these tools quickly.
- **Tool Handle Options**: Located next to the transform tools, these icons let you choose between local and global space for transformations, affecting how objects rotate and move relative to their orientation or the world grid.

7. Additional Panels: Animation, Animator, and Asset Store

Unity includes several additional panels that provide specialized functionality for more advanced aspects of game development.

- **Animation Panel**: The Animation panel allows you to create and edit animations directly within Unity. For example, you can create animations for a character's walking and jumping motions by keyframing properties like position and rotation. The Animation panel is essential for creating fluid, engaging animations without requiring external software.

- **Animator Panel**: The Animator panel is used to control complex animation behaviors and transitions. It allows you to create a "state machine" where different animations are linked together with rules for transitioning between them. This panel is particularly useful for character animations, where a character's state may change based on conditions like speed, health, or player input.
- **Asset Store Panel**: Unity's Asset Store provides a vast library of resources, including models, textures, scripts, and sound effects. This panel allows you to search for and purchase assets without leaving the Unity Editor, saving time and effort. The Asset Store is especially valuable for beginners who may need high-quality assets to speed up development.

8. Customizing the Unity Interface

Unity's interface is highly customizable, allowing you to arrange panels according to your preferences and workflow.

- **Docking and Rearranging Panels**: You can drag and dock panels to different areas of the screen, creating custom layouts. Unity also offers preset layouts (e.g., "Default," "2 by 3," "Tall") accessible from the top-right corner, which cater to different types of projects.
- **Saving Custom Layouts**: After arranging the panels to your liking, you can save the custom layout by going to **Window > Layouts > Save Layout**. This saves time by allowing you to quickly revert to your preferred setup if you adjust the layout for specific tasks.
- **Full-Screen Mode**: Unity supports a full-screen mode for individual panels, which you can activate by pressing Shift + Space while hovering over a panel. This is helpful for focusing on specific tasks, such as

maximizing the Scene View for level design or the Inspector for detailed adjustments.

Mastering the Unity Interface for Efficient Development

Understanding Unity's key panels and tools is essential for a smooth development process. The Scene and Game Views provide visual control, while the Hierarchy and Inspector panels help you manage and adjust your GameObjects efficiently. The Console panel serves as a powerful debugging tool, and the Project panel organizes all assets in your project.

By navigating Unity's interface with ease, you can focus on building your game without being hindered by technical complexities. The Unity Editor offers a powerful yet flexible environment, and mastering it will make you a more proficient and effective game developer.

Introduction to the Unity Documentation and Community

Unity's extensive documentation and its active, supportive community are invaluable resources for game developers at every skill level. These resources not only provide technical explanations and tutorials but also foster a collaborative environment where developers can learn from each other, solve problems together, and share creative ideas. This section introduces the Unity documentation and community platforms, offering insights on how to maximize these resources to accelerate your learning and enhance your development skills.

1. Unity Documentation: The Definitive Guide to Unity's Features

The official Unity documentation is a comprehensive online resource covering every aspect of Unity's functionality. From basic interface guides to complex API references, Unity's documentation provides in-depth explanations and examples, making it an essential tool for beginners and experienced developers alike.

- **Accessing the Documentation**: The documentation is accessible directly within the Unity Editor via **Help > Unity Manual** or **Help > Scripting API**. These links open the official documentation in a web browser, giving you immediate access to details about any component, feature, or scripting API in Unity.
- **Unity Manual**: The Unity Manual is structured like a user's guide, introducing Unity's features, workflows, and development best practices. It covers topics such as:
- **Getting Started**: An introduction to Unity's interface, panels, and tools, helping new users navigate the Editor effectively.
- **Asset Management**: Guides on importing, organizing, and optimizing assets within Unity, including file formats and best practices.
- **Graphics and Visual Effects**: Detailed explanations on using Unity's rendering pipelines, lighting systems, materials, and shaders.
- **Physics, Animation, and Audio**: Instructions on creating realistic physical interactions, animations, and audio effects.
- **Platform-Specific Development**: Platform-specific settings and optimizations for building games on mobile, console, PC, and WebGL.
- **Unity Scripting API**: The Scripting API documentation is a technical reference for Unity's extensive C# API, which allows you to implement everything from basic gameplay mechanics to complex systems. Key elements of the Scripting API documentation include:
- **Classes and Functions**: Each Unity class, such as GameObject, Transform, and Rigidbody, has dedicated pages detailing properties, methods, and events associated with it.
- **Example Code Snippets**: Most API entries include example code snippets demonstrating common uses and best practices. These snippets are useful for understanding how to structure your code and integrate Unity's functionality.
- **Version-Specific Information**: The API documentation includes notes on deprecated functions and version-specific changes, helping you write code compatible with different Unity versions.
- **Search and Navigation**: Unity's documentation includes a powerful

search feature, allowing you to quickly locate relevant information. For instance, if you're unsure how to use the Rigidbody component, searching for "Rigidbody" in the documentation brings up a list of related topics, including component settings, physics interactions, and scripting examples.

2. Unity Learn: Structured Learning Paths and Tutorials

Unity Learn is an official education platform that offers structured learning paths, tutorials, and interactive projects. Designed for developers of all experience levels, Unity Learn provides a well-rounded foundation in Unity's core features and workflows.

- **Learning Pathways**: Unity Learn includes curated learning pathways for different types of users, such as **Beginner, Intermediate,** and **Advanced** tracks. Each pathway consists of tutorials, videos, quizzes, and exercises designed to build skills progressively. For instance:
- **Creator Pathway**: Covers the basics of Unity and game design, aimed at beginners who want to explore Unity's possibilities.
- **Programmer Pathway**: A more coding-focused track, covering scripting and logic in Unity. This pathway is ideal for those looking to build a solid foundation in Unity C# scripting.
- **Artist Pathway**: Focuses on visual elements, such as asset creation, lighting, and shaders, helping artists bring their ideas to life in Unity.
- **Interactive Projects and Challenges**: Many Unity Learn courses include interactive challenges, where you apply what you've learned in small, manageable projects. These challenges reinforce skills and allow you to explore different aspects of game development, such as creating a simple 2D platformer or building a 3D maze.
- **Certifications**: Unity Learn also offers certifications that validate your proficiency in specific areas, such as the **Unity Certified User** and **Unity Certified Programmer** credentials. These certifications can enhance your resume, showcasing your Unity skills to potential employers or collaborators.

3. **Unity Community: Forums, Answers, and Groups**

Unity's community is one of its greatest assets, consisting of developers, artists, and hobbyists who are passionate about sharing their knowledge and supporting each other. Through forums, Q&A platforms, and social groups, Unity's community fosters an open and collaborative environment that helps developers troubleshoot issues, learn new techniques, and stay inspired.

- **Unity Forums**: The Unity Forums are divided into categories for different aspects of development, including general discussion, scripting, graphics, and platform-specific questions. The forums offer:
- **Problem Solving and Feedback**: Developers often post questions about specific issues they're facing, from error messages to design challenges. Other users respond with solutions, tips, and advice, creating a collaborative learning environment.
- **Showcase and Feedback**: Many forum sections allow developers to showcase their projects and receive constructive feedback from peers. This is a great way to gain insights and improve your work while sharing your progress with a supportive community.
- **Asset Store Announcements**: Unity asset creators often announce new tools and assets on the forums, providing a first look at resources that can enhance your projects.
- **Unity Answers**: Unity Answers is a Q&A platform similar to Stack Overflow, where developers can post questions and receive answers from the community. Topics range from basic scripting questions to complex problems in physics, UI design, and optimization.
- **Searchable Database**: Unity Answers is a vast, searchable database of previously asked questions, making it a valuable resource when troubleshooting issues. Often, someone else has already encountered (and solved) the same issue you're facing.
- **Voting and Accepted Answers**: Users can vote on answers, and question posters can mark the best answer as "accepted." This voting system helps highlight the most accurate and helpful responses, saving

time when searching for solutions.

- **Unity Discord and Facebook Groups**: Discord servers and Facebook groups provide real-time, interactive communities where Unity developers connect, share knowledge, and collaborate.
- **Networking Opportunities**: These groups are great for networking with other Unity developers, finding collaborators, and even discovering freelance or job opportunities.
- **Specialized Communities**: Many groups focus on specific aspects of Unity development, such as VR/AR development, asset creation, or mobile optimization. This makes it easier to find advice tailored to your needs.

4. The Asset Store: Enhancing Your Projects with Community-Created Resources

Unity's Asset Store is an expansive marketplace for assets, including models, textures, scripts, audio, animations, and tools created by the Unity community. The Asset Store is an invaluable resource for both beginners and experienced developers, offering high-quality assets that can speed up development or provide inspiration for your own work.

- **Free and Paid Assets**: The Asset Store includes both free and paid assets, allowing developers on any budget to access useful resources. Free assets are a great way for beginners to start experimenting without an investment, while paid assets often include detailed models, polished animations, or advanced tools that can elevate the quality of your project.
- **Popular Asset Categories**:
- **3D Models**: Characters, environments, props, and vehicles that you can customize or use directly in your scenes.
- **2D Assets**: Sprites, icons, and tilemaps for 2D games, providing visually consistent sets for platformers, puzzle games, and more.
- **Scripts and Tools**: Plugins and scripts that expand Unity's functionality, such as advanced physics systems, animation tools, and AI systems.

- **Audio Assets**: Sound effects, music tracks, and ambient audio that enhance the atmosphere and immersion of your game.
- **Using and Modifying Assets**: Once downloaded, assets can be modified, customized, or combined with other elements in your project. This flexibility allows you to use assets as a foundation and adapt them to fit your vision.
- **Subscription-Based Packages (Unity Pro and Unity Plus)**: Unity offers subscription-based packages with additional benefits, such as advanced Asset Store discounts, priority support, and access to Unity-exclusive tools. For professional developers and studios, these packages can provide value and exclusive resources that enhance productivity.

5. Unity's Support and Troubleshooting Resources

Beyond the documentation and community forums, Unity offers official support and troubleshooting resources to assist you in resolving more complex issues.

- **Unity Issue Tracker**: Unity's Issue Tracker lists known bugs, issues, and resolutions for different versions of Unity. If you encounter a recurring bug or unusual behavior, checking the Issue Tracker can reveal whether it's a known issue and if a fix or workaround is available.
- **Release Notes and Upgrade Guides**: Unity's release notes detail changes, improvements, and fixes in each version update, helping developers understand how updates might impact their projects. Upgrade guides also provide specific steps for transitioning projects between Unity versions, helping you avoid compatibility issues.
- **Unity Support Plans**: For developers working on professional or mission-critical projects, Unity offers support plans with varying levels of assistance. Unity Plus, Pro, and Enterprise plans include access to priority support, enabling faster responses to technical questions and troubleshooting needs.

6. Staying Up-to-Date with Unity's Community and Development

The game development landscape is constantly evolving, with Unity regularly introducing new features, tools, and updates. Staying connected with Unity's community and official announcements helps you remain informed about changes that can impact your projects.

- **Unity Blog**: The Unity Blog provides news on engine updates, feature releases, developer spotlights, and industry trends. It's an excellent resource for staying informed about upcoming features, tools, and best practices.
- **Unity Events and Conferences**: Unity hosts online and in-person events, such as **Unite**, where developers gather to learn from industry experts, network, and discover Unity's latest tools and innovations. These events often feature talks, workshops, and panel discussions, providing valuable learning opportunities.
- **Social Media and Newsletters**: Unity maintains active social media accounts, including Twitter, Facebook, and YouTube, where they post news, tutorials, and community showcases. Subscribing to Unity's newsletter ensures you receive regular updates, announcements, and curated content directly in your inbox.

Leveraging Unity's Documentation and Community for Success

Unity's documentation and community resources provide everything you need to grow as a developer, troubleshoot issues, and refine your skills. The documentation and scripting API serve as a complete technical reference, while Unity Learn offers structured learning paths. The forums, Unity Answers, and social media groups enable real-time interaction, connecting you with other developers who can help you overcome challenges and expand your knowledge.

How to Use This Book: Projects, Exercises, and Resources

This book is designed as a practical guide to learning Unity and C# through hands-on experience, progressive exercises, and real-world projects. Each chapter introduces core concepts, followed by exercises and projects that reinforce the material through active practice. This approach allows you to build knowledge step-by-step, mastering each concept before moving on to more complex topics. This section outlines how to make the most of the book's structure, projects, exercises, and additional resources to ensure you have a well-rounded and comprehensive learning experience.

1. Structure of Each Chapter: Concept to Application

Each chapter in this book is crafted to take you from understanding basic concepts to applying them in real-world scenarios. This progression enables you to learn by doing, which is one of the most effective methods for skill acquisition in game development.

- **Conceptual Explanations**: Chapters start with an introduction to the main topic, explaining essential concepts, definitions, and their practical uses within Unity. These explanations provide a foundation for understanding the "why" and "how" behind each tool, feature, or function.
- **Code and Examples**: Key concepts are reinforced with code examples and visual demonstrations that illustrate their practical applications. These examples serve as references for structuring your own code and applying Unity's components effectively.
- **Hands-On Exercises**: After learning the basics, you'll find exercises that encourage you to experiment with the concepts. These exercises vary in difficulty, challenging you to explore different facets of Unity and C# while reinforcing your understanding.
- **Cumulative Projects**: At the end of major sections, the book introduces cumulative projects that combine multiple concepts from previous chapters. These projects are designed to simulate real-world game development scenarios, helping you integrate and apply what you've learned in a meaningful way.

2. Exercises: Reinforce Your Skills Through Practice

Exercises in this book are structured to encourage exploration and experimentation, helping you solidify your understanding of each chapter's content.

- **Short Exercises**: Most chapters contain shorter exercises focused on a specific concept or skill. These tasks are designed to reinforce what you've just learned without overwhelming you, allowing you to focus on mastering one small skill at a time.
- **Exploratory Prompts**: Some exercises prompt you to experiment with variations on the presented code or try different settings in Unity. These exploratory prompts are intended to build confidence in modifying code, working with GameObjects, and navigating Unity's interface.
- **Self-Check Questions**: Many chapters include self-check questions that encourage you to review key concepts before moving forward. These questions help you assess your understanding and highlight areas that might need additional review.

3. Projects: Applying Your Knowledge in Real-World Scenarios

Projects are the cornerstone of this book's learning approach, providing opportunities to apply multiple concepts within a cohesive structure. Each project is carefully designed to mirror real-world game development tasks, giving you practical experience in Unity's workflow and C# coding.

- **Progressive Complexity**: Projects start simple, allowing you to build foundational skills before tackling more challenging tasks. Early projects might involve creating a basic 2D game, such as a clicker or platformer, while later projects focus on 3D game mechanics, user interfaces, or implementing sound and physics.
- **Realistic Game Scenarios**: Projects simulate real-world game development by involving planning, design, scripting, and testing. You'll practice essential skills like character movement, collision detection, score tracking, and UI creation, providing a realistic sense of the

development process.

- **Capstone Projects**: Toward the end of the book, you'll find more complex capstone projects that integrate everything you've learned. These projects serve as a final challenge, helping you combine skills and concepts into a cohesive game. Completing these capstone projects will give you a portfolio-worthy piece that showcases your Unity skills to potential employers or collaborators.

4. Resources: Supplementary Tools and References

In addition to the book's content, a range of supplementary resources is provided to support your learning journey. These resources include additional readings, downloadable assets, and links to external learning tools that will enhance your understanding of Unity and C#.

- **Downloadable Project Files**: Each chapter includes downloadable assets and project files, which allow you to follow along with the examples and exercises. These files include starter assets, scripts, and prefabs, providing a quick start and helping you save time on routine tasks.
- **Recommended Documentation and Guides**: Throughout the book, you'll find links to Unity's official documentation, online forums, and learning guides. These resources offer further explanation and examples, giving you a broader perspective on each topic.
- **Video Tutorials and Interactive Courses**: In sections covering complex topics, video tutorials are suggested to provide visual demonstrations of specific workflows. Interactive courses and challenges on Unity Learn are also recommended for areas that benefit from hands-on practice and step-by-step guidance.
- **Community Platforms for Troubleshooting**: If you encounter a particularly challenging concept or error, the book directs you to Unity's community forums, Unity Answers, and other collaborative platforms where you can seek guidance from experienced developers.

5. Troubleshooting and Debugging Tips

Troubleshooting and debugging are vital skills in game development, as encountering and resolving issues is a natural part of the development process. Each chapter includes tips for identifying and fixing common problems, helping you build confidence in debugging.

- **Common Errors**: Throughout the book, common errors associated with specific topics are discussed, along with steps for resolving them. For example, you might encounter syntax errors, null reference exceptions, or object collisions that don't behave as expected. These error explanations provide insights into how Unity and C# function, making it easier to understand the cause and solution.

- **Debugging Techniques**: Unity's Console panel and Visual Studio debugging tools are covered extensively, allowing you to learn best practices for tracking variables, catching errors, and analyzing the behavior of your code. Debugging tips are included in each chapter, particularly in areas where errors are likely to occur, such as scripting and physics.

6. Learning Through Iteration and Experimentation

Game development is an iterative process, where ideas are prototyped, tested, refined, and polished over multiple stages. This book encourages a similar iterative approach, prompting you to experiment, revisit, and improve upon your work as you learn.

- **Prototype and Refine**: Each project includes opportunities to experiment with different values, settings, and code variations, allowing you to understand how small changes impact gameplay. Prototyping and refining your work will teach you to approach game design as an iterative process, improving your problem-solving and critical thinking skills.

- **Experiment with Customization**: Exercises encourage customization, such as modifying colors, movement speeds, or object behaviors.

35

By experimenting with different configurations, you gain a deeper understanding of Unity's flexibility and learn how to tailor mechanics to fit your unique vision.

- **Challenge Yourself with Extensions**: Many chapters include optional "Challenge Yourself" sections with advanced tasks or variations on the main exercises. These challenges encourage you to apply your knowledge creatively, helping you explore Unity's capabilities beyond the basic examples.

7. Building a Portfolio of Work

This book is designed to help you develop practical skills that you can showcase through a portfolio of work. By completing the projects and exercises, you'll create a range of games and interactive experiences that demonstrate your abilities in Unity and C#.

- **Saving Project Snapshots**: As you work on projects, consider saving snapshots of each version. This way, you'll have a record of your progress and the ability to revert to previous versions if needed. These snapshots also serve as a portfolio of your work, showing your growth as a developer.

- **Showcasing Capstone Projects**: The final projects in this book are intended to be polished, fully functional games that you can showcase in your portfolio. Including these projects in your portfolio demonstrates your ability to design, code, and execute a complete game concept, which can be valuable when applying for internships, jobs, or freelance projects.

- **Additional Resources for Portfolio Development**: Throughout the book, resources for creating a professional portfolio, such as project presentation tips and GitHub basics, are included. These resources help you organize and present your work effectively to potential employers or collaborators.

8. Getting the Most Out of This Book

To maximize the learning experience, consider the following tips as you work through the chapters:

- **Pace Yourself**: Learning game development takes time and practice, so take each chapter step-by-step. It's normal to revisit chapters and exercises multiple times to reinforce your understanding, especially when building new skills.
- **Engage Actively with the Exercises**: The exercises are designed to encourage hands-on learning. Approach each exercise as an opportunity to explore, experiment, and understand, rather than merely completing the steps. The more actively you engage with the material, the more effective your learning will be.
- **Seek Help When Needed**: Don't hesitate to seek help if you encounter challenges. Unity's documentation, forums, and the community resources mentioned in this book are invaluable support systems. Learning to troubleshoot effectively is a key skill in game development, and reaching out to the community can help you overcome obstacles faster.
- **Take Notes and Reflect**: Taking notes as you progress through each chapter helps reinforce concepts and serves as a personal reference guide. Reflecting on what you've learned after completing a chapter or project helps consolidate your understanding and prepares you for the next steps.

A Practical Guide to Mastering Unity and C#

This book provides a structured, hands-on approach to learning Unity and C#, taking you from the basics to building fully functional games. By combining theory with exercises, projects, and practical applications, it equips you with the knowledge and skills to develop your own games confidently. From foundational coding principles to advanced game mechanics, each chapter builds on the previous one, guiding you toward mastery of Unity's diverse tools and capabilities.

Foundations of C# Programming for Unity

Basics of C#: Syntax and Structure

C# (C-sharp) is a popular programming language developed by Microsoft, known for its clear, structured syntax and wide applications in game development, particularly in Unity. It's a strongly-typed, object-oriented language, meaning every variable must have a defined type, and it uses a structure that organizes code into objects and classes, making it easier to manage and scale. Understanding C# syntax and structure is essential as it forms the backbone of Unity scripting, enabling developers to create behaviors and control game logic effectively.

What is C#? An Overview for New Developers

C# is an object-oriented, strongly-typed language that focuses on making code readable and maintainable. It's particularly suited to Unity due to its stability, versatility, and high compatibility with Unity's component-based architecture.

Key Characteristics of C#:

- **Object-Oriented Programming (OOP)**: C# is organized around objects, which allows you to model real-world entities in code. In Unity, this approach enables you to manage complex systems by structuring your code into objects that represent players, enemies, items, and other game elements.

- **Strongly Typed Language**: C# requires each variable to have a specific data type (like int or string), making code predictable and preventing many common errors.
- **Cross-Platform**: With .NET and Mono, C# code can run across multiple platforms, allowing Unity projects to deploy on PC, mobile, consoles, and WebGL without major modifications.
- **Interoperability with Visual Studio**: C# works seamlessly with Visual Studio, a powerful Integrated Development Environment (IDE) that provides debugging, error-checking, and IntelliSense, making it easy to code and troubleshoot.

Why Use C# in Unity?

- **Readability and Efficiency**: C#'s syntax is clean and easy to read, making it suitable for developers at all levels. The language's straightforward structure allows beginners to get up to speed quickly, while advanced developers benefit from robust libraries and frameworks.
- **Component-Based Structure in Unity**: C# integrates smoothly with Unity's component system, where each script attached to a GameObject controls specific behaviors. This allows for a modular approach to game development, where scripts are reusable and easy to manage.

Real-World Application:

- In Unity, you'll use C# to write scripts that control object behaviors, handle player inputs, trigger animations, and manage game logic. This language empowers developers to create complex game mechanics without having to reinvent basic functionalities.

Writing Your First C# Program: Syntax and Basic Structure

To begin scripting in Unity, let's start with a simple "Hello, World!" program in C#. This basic example demonstrates the core structure and syntax used in C#.

Setting Up a Script in Unity:

- **Create a Script**: In Unity's Project panel, right-click, select **Create > C# Script**, and name it HelloWorld.
- **Open the Script**: Double-click the HelloWorld script to open it in Visual Studio. You'll see Unity's default script structure, which includes basic methods and libraries.

Exploring the Default Structure:

```csharp
using System.Collections;
using System.Collections.Generic;
using UnityEngine;

public class HelloWorld : MonoBehaviour
{
    // Start is called before the first frame update
    void Start()
    {
        Debug.Log("Hello, World!");
    }

    // Update is called once per frame
    void Update()
    {
    }
}
```

Here's a breakdown of this structure:

- **Using Statements**: The using keywords import libraries that provide essential functions for Unity scripting. using UnityEngine; allows access to Unity's core functionalities, such as GameObject manipulation, physics, and input handling.
- **Class Definition**: public class HelloWorld : MonoBehaviour declares a

class named HelloWorld, which inherits from MonoBehaviour, Unity's base class for all scripts attached to GameObjects.

- **Start Method**: void Start() is a built-in method that runs once when the GameObject is activated. It's commonly used to initialize variables or set up initial states.
- **Update Method**: void Update() is called once per frame, making it ideal for code that needs to update continuously, such as movement or animation control.
- **Debug.Log**: Debug.Log("Hello, World!"); sends a message to Unity's Console, useful for testing and debugging.

Running the Script in Unity:

- **Attach to GameObject**: Drag the HelloWorld script onto any GameObject in the Scene.
- **Play the Scene**: Click the Play button in Unity. The Console should display "Hello, World!" indicating that the script executed successfully.

Variables, Data Types, and Operators

Variables and data types are essential in C# as they enable you to store, manipulate, and work with different types of data. Operators allow you to perform operations on this data, forming the building blocks for all programming logic.

Variables:

Variables in C# store data values. Each variable has a data type, a name, and a value. Here's a simple declaration:

```csharp
int score = 0;
string playerName = "Hero";
bool isGameOver = false;
```

- **Naming Conventions**: Use camelCase for variable names (e.g., player-Health, enemyCount) to enhance readability and follow C# standards.

Data Types:

C# includes several primary data types, each suited for storing different types of information.

Integer (int): Holds whole numbers, positive or negative.

```csharp
int playerScore = 100;
```

Float (float) and Double (double): Store decimal numbers. float takes less memory than double but is less precise. Floats require an "f" suffix.

```csharp
float speed = 4.5f;
double preciseValue = 3.14159;
```

String (string): Stores sequences of characters (text), enclosed in double quotes.

```csharp
string message = "Welcome to Unity!";
```

Boolean (bool): Holds true or false values, useful in conditions and states.

```csharp
bool isAlive = true;
```

Character (char): Stores a single character, enclosed in single quotes.

```csharp
char grade = 'A';
```

Operators:

Operators allow you to perform calculations and compare values.

Arithmetic Operators:

- + (Addition), - (Subtraction), * (Multiplication), / (Division), % (Modulus - remainder).

```csharp
int totalScore = 50 + 25;
int difference = 100 - 25;
float average = totalScore / 2.0f;
```

Comparison Operators: Used to compare values, returning a boolean result.

- == (Equal), != (Not Equal), > (Greater), < (Less), >= (Greater or Equal), <= (Less or Equal).

```csharp
bool isHighScore = (playerScore > 100);
```

Logical Operators: Used to combine or invert boolean expressions.

- && (AND), || (OR), ! (NOT).

```
csharp

bool canPlay = (isAlive && !isGameOver);
```

Examples of Variables and Operators in Action

Here's a practical example that combines variables and operators:

```csharp
csharp

public class GameStats : MonoBehaviour
{
    int playerHealth = 100;
    int damage = 20;
    bool isPlayerAlive = true;

    void TakeDamage()
    {
        playerHealth -= damage;
        if (playerHealth <= 0)
        {
            isPlayerAlive = false;
            Debug.Log("Player is defeated!");
        }
        else
        {
            Debug.Log("Player health: " + playerHealth);
        }
    }
}
```

In this script:

- **playerHealth** and **damage** are integer variables representing the player's health and damage taken.
- The **TakeDamage** method subtracts damage from playerHealth and checks if playerHealth is zero or below. If true, isPlayerAlive is set to

false, ending the game.

This foundational understanding of C# syntax and structure, variables, data types, and operators provides a strong start for scripting in Unity. As you progress, these concepts will become essential in building game mechanics, handling object states, and creating complex game logic. In Unity, these programming basics empower you to bring your ideas to life, with each line of code adding to the interactivity and depth of your game world.

Control Flow and Logic

Control flow and logic are fundamental concepts in programming that allow developers to dictate the order in which code executes. Through conditional statements and loops, C# enables developers to make decisions within the program and repeat specific actions based on conditions. These concepts are especially important in game development, where you'll often need to control behaviors based on player input, game states, and real-time conditions. In Unity, control flow structures allow you to design complex gameplay mechanics, AI behaviors, and event-driven interactions.

Conditional Statements: if, else, and switch

Conditional statements allow you to control the flow of your program by executing code only if certain conditions are met. In game development, you might use conditionals to check if a player has enough health to continue, if an enemy is within range to attack, or if the game should transition to the next level.

if and else Statements

The if statement is the most basic form of conditional logic, allowing code to execute only if a specified condition is true. If the condition is false, the program skips over the if block. You can also use else and else if to handle multiple conditions.

Syntax of if Statements:

```
csharp

if (condition)
{
    // Code to execute if condition is true
}
```

For example:

```
csharp

int playerHealth = 50;

if (playerHealth > 0)
{
    Debug.Log("Player is still alive!");
}
```

Using else and else if:

- **else**: Executes a block of code if the if condition is false.
- **else if**: Allows multiple conditions to be checked sequentially.

Example:

```
csharp

int playerHealth = 20;

if (playerHealth > 50)
{
    Debug.Log("Player is in good health.");
}
else if (playerHealth > 0)
{
```

```
    Debug.Log("Player is wounded.");
}
else
{
    Debug.Log("Player is defeated.");
}
```

In this example, if playerHealth is greater than 50, the player is in good health. If it's between 1 and 50, they're wounded. If it's 0 or less, the player is defeated.

switch Statement

The switch statement is an alternative to multiple if-else conditions and is often used when there are several possible values for a single variable. The switch statement matches a variable against different cases and executes the corresponding block of code.

Syntax of switch:

```csharp
switch (variable)
{
    case value1:
        // Code for case 1
        break;
    case value2:
        // Code for case 2
        break;
    default:
        // Code if no cases match
        break;
}
```

Example in Game Development:

```
csharp

int weaponType = 1;

switch (weaponType)
{
    case 1:
        Debug.Log("Sword equipped.");
        break;
    case 2:
        Debug.Log("Bow equipped.");
        break;
    case 3:
        Debug.Log("Magic Staff equipped.");
        break;
    default:
        Debug.Log("No weapon equipped.");
        break;
}
```

In this example, depending on the value of weaponType, the script logs the appropriate message to the Console. The default case handles any undefined values.

Loops: for, while, and foreach

Loops allow you to repeat a block of code multiple times, often until a specific condition is met. In game development, loops are used for tasks like spawning multiple enemies, updating game states over time, or iterating through a list of items.

for Loop

The for loop is commonly used when you know the exact number of iterations in advance. It's structured with an initializer, condition, and iterator, making it ideal for counting or processing items in an array.

Syntax of for Loop:

```csharp

for (initializer; condition; iterator)
{
    // Code to execute in each iteration
}
```

Example in Game Development:

```csharp

for (int i = 0; i < 5; i++)
{
    Debug.Log("Enemy " + i + " spawned.");
}
```

This loop logs a message five times, indicating that five enemies have been spawned. The variable i starts at 0, increments by 1 each time (i++), and stops once i reaches 5.

while Loop

The while loop is used when the number of iterations is not predetermined and the loop continues until a specific condition becomes false.

Syntax of while Loop:

```csharp

while (condition)
{
    // Code to execute as long as condition is true
}
```

Example in Game Development:

```
csharp

int playerHealth = 100;

while (playerHealth > 0)
{
    playerHealth -= 10;
    Debug.Log("Player takes damage. Health: " + playerHealth);
}
```

In this example, the player's health decreases by 10 each loop iteration until it reaches 0. The loop stops once playerHealth is no longer greater than 0.

foreach Loop

The foreach loop is specifically designed for iterating over collections, like arrays or lists. It simplifies looping through all items in a collection without needing an index.

Syntax of foreach Loop:

```
csharp

foreach (var item in collection)
{
    // Code to execute for each item
}
```

Example in Game Development:

```
csharp

string[] inventory = { "Sword", "Shield", "Potion" };

foreach (string item in inventory)
{
    Debug.Log("Inventory item: " + item);
```

```
}
```

This loop iterates over each element in the inventory array, logging each item to the Console. The foreach loop automatically retrieves each item in the collection without needing an index.

Putting It All Together: Example of Control Flow and Logic in Game Development

Here's a more comprehensive example demonstrating if statements and loops within a game scenario:

```csharp
public class Player : MonoBehaviour
{
    int playerHealth = 100;
    string[] inventory = { "Sword", "Shield", "Potion" };

    void CheckHealth()
    {
        if (playerHealth > 70)
        {
            Debug.Log("Player is healthy.");
        }
        else if (playerHealth > 30)
        {
            Debug.Log("Player is injured.");
        }
        else
        {
            Debug.Log("Player is critically injured!");
        }
    }

    void DisplayInventory()
    {
        foreach (string item in inventory)
```

```
        {
            Debug.Log("Inventory: " + item);
        }
    }

    void TakeDamage(int damage)
    {
        playerHealth -= damage;

        if (playerHealth <= 0)
        {
            Debug.Log("Game Over. Player has been defeated.");
            playerHealth = 0;
        }
        else
        {
            Debug.Log("Player health: " + playerHealth);
        }
    }

    void Start()
    {
        // Example usage
        CheckHealth();
        DisplayInventory();

        for (int i = 0; i < 3; i++)
        {
            TakeDamage(25);
        }
    }
}
```

In this script:

- **CheckHealth()** uses if, else if, and else statements to determine and log the player's health status.
- **DisplayInventory()** uses a foreach loop to log each item in the player's inventory.

- **TakeDamage()** reduces playerHealth by a specified amount and checks if health is below or equal to zero, logging "Game Over" if the player is defeated.
- The **Start()** method demonstrates the usage of a for loop to call TakeDamage() multiple times, simulating repeated hits on the player.

Understanding control flow and logic in C# is crucial for designing interactive and dynamic gameplay experiences. Conditionals (if, else, switch) enable your code to make decisions, while loops (for, while, foreach) allow for repeated actions, such as spawning objects or updating game states. By mastering these concepts, you'll gain the flexibility to build engaging mechanics and responsive systems within Unity. These tools are foundational as you progress in your game development journey, enabling you to manage game logic and behavior in an organized and efficient manner.

Functions and Methods

Functions and methods are essential elements in programming, providing a structured way to group code into reusable blocks that perform specific tasks. In C#, functions and methods are technically the same concept; however, methods are functions that belong to a class, which is the primary context for code in C#. By using methods, you can break down complex tasks into smaller, more manageable pieces, improving code readability and reusability. This section explores how to define, call, and use methods effectively in Unity.

Defining and Calling Functions

In C#, a method is a block of code that performs a specific action. You can define a method once and call it multiple times within your program, making it useful for repetitive tasks. Every method in C# has a specific structure that includes a return type, name, parameters, and the body of the method.

Syntax of a Method

Here's the basic structure of a method in C#:

```csharp
returnType MethodName(parameters)
{
    // Code to execute
}
```

Return Type: Specifies the type of value the method will return. If the method doesn't return a value, the return type is void.

Method Name: The identifier for the method, used to call it from other parts of your program.

Parameters: Optional values passed to the method when it's called, enclosed in parentheses.

Method Body: The code that the method will execute, enclosed in curly braces { }.

Example: Defining a Simple Method

Below is an example of a method that prints a greeting message to the Console:

```csharp
void GreetPlayer()
{
    Debug.Log("Welcome to the game!");
}
```

In this example:

- void indicates that the method doesn't return a value.
- GreetPlayer is the name of the method.

- The method contains a single line of code that uses Debug.Log() to print a message to Unity's Console.

Calling a Method

To execute a method, you call it by writing its name followed by parentheses. If the method has parameters, you include them within the parentheses.

```csharp
GreetPlayer(); // Calls the GreetPlayer method
```

To see this in action in Unity, you could call GreetPlayer() from the Start() method in a script:

```csharp
void Start()
{
    GreetPlayer(); // Calls the GreetPlayer method when the game
    starts
}
```

When you run the game in Unity, the Console will display "Welcome to the game!" indicating that the method was called successfully.

Parameter Passing

Parameters are values you pass into a method to customize its behavior. By using parameters, you can make methods more flexible and reusable, as they can operate on different values without needing to rewrite the code.

Defining Parameters

Parameters are defined within the parentheses in the method's signature. Each parameter has a data type and a name, separated by a space. If a method has multiple parameters, you separate them with commas.

```csharp
void GreetPlayerByName(string playerName)
{
    Debug.Log("Hello, " + playerName + "!");
}
```

In this example, GreetPlayerByName takes one parameter of type string named playerName. When this method is called, you provide a name that will be used in the greeting.

Calling a Method with Parameters

When you call a method with parameters, you must provide values (known as arguments) that match the method's parameters.

```csharp
GreetPlayerByName("Alice"); // Outputs "Hello, Alice!"
GreetPlayerByName("Bob");   // Outputs "Hello, Bob!"
```

This makes the method more versatile, as you can call it with different names without changing the code within the method.

Multiple Parameters

A method can have multiple parameters, allowing it to accept a range of values. Here's an example that takes a player's name and score as parameters:

```csharp
void DisplayScore(string playerName, int score)
{
    Debug.Log(playerName + " scored " + score + " points!");
}
```

To call DisplayScore, provide both a name and a score:

```csharp
DisplayScore("Alice", 100);   // Outputs "Alice scored 100 points!"
DisplayScore("Bob", 75);      // Outputs "Bob scored 75 points!"
```

This method is flexible and can display scores for any player by using different arguments.

Return Values

Methods can also return a value to the code that called them. The return value allows you to obtain the result of a calculation or operation performed within the method.

Defining a Method with a Return Value

When a method returns a value, you replace void with the appropriate return type and use the return keyword to specify the value to return.

```csharp
int CalculateScore(int kills, int bonus)
{
    int score = (kills * 10) + bonus;
    return score;
}
```

In this example:

- int is the return type, meaning CalculateScore will return an integer value.
- The return statement sends the score variable's value back to wherever the method was called.

Calling a Method with a Return Value

When calling a method that returns a value, you can store the result in a variable or use it directly.

```csharp
int playerScore = CalculateScore(5, 20); // playerScore is 70
Debug.Log("Final Score: " + playerScore); // Outputs "Final
Score: 70"
```

Here, CalculateScore(5, 20) returns a score of 70, which is then stored in playerScore. This approach is useful for complex calculations or logic that needs to be reusable across multiple parts of a program.

Example: Combining Parameters and Return Values in Unity

Let's look at a more comprehensive example that uses parameters and return values within a Unity context.

```csharp
public class Player : MonoBehaviour
{
    int baseHealth = 100;

    int CalculateDamage(int attackPower, int enemyDefense)
    {
        int damage = (attackPower - enemyDefense);
        if (damage < 0)
        {
            damage = 0; // Prevents negative damage
        }
        return damage;
    }

    void TakeDamage(int damage)
    {
        baseHealth -= damage;
        if (baseHealth <= 0)
        {
```

```
        Debug.Log("Player defeated!");
    }
    else
    {
        Debug.Log("Player health: " + baseHealth);
    }
}

void Start()
{
    int damageTaken = CalculateDamage(30, 10); // attackPower
    = 30, enemyDefense = 10
    TakeDamage(damageTaken); // Reduces baseHealth by
    damageTaken
}
}
```

CalculateDamage Method:

- This method takes attackPower and enemyDefense as parameters.
- It calculates damage based on the difference between attackPower and enemyDefense.
- If the calculated damage is less than zero, it sets damage to 0 to avoid negative damage.
- Finally, it returns the calculated damage.

TakeDamage Method:

- Takes damage as a parameter and reduces baseHealth by this amount.
- If baseHealth drops to 0 or below, the player is considered defeated.

Start Method:

- Calls CalculateDamage with specific values for attackPower and enemyDefense.
- Stores the returned damageTaken value and passes it to TakeDamage.

This example demonstrates how parameters and return values enable reusable, organized code. By isolating the damage calculation in CalculateDamage, you can reuse it for any attack in your game.

Methods are powerful tools in C#, allowing you to organize, reuse, and extend your code. Understanding how to define and call methods, use parameters, and return values will enable you to build more sophisticated game mechanics in Unity. These foundational skills help you write modular code that's easy to manage, test, and adapt, making your scripts more robust and flexible as you develop complex interactions and behaviors.

Object-Oriented Programming Concepts for Game Development

Object-Oriented Programming (OOP) is central to designing structured, reusable code, especially for complex projects like games. OOP allows developers to create modular components that can be used across various game elements. In Unity, OOP concepts help manage and organize gameplay mechanics through classes and objects, inheritance, polymorphism, and encapsulation. Understanding these concepts is essential to creating scalable, maintainable game code that enhances the efficiency and versatility of your development process.

Classes and Objects: Building Blocks for Games

In OOP, classes and objects are fundamental. A **class** is a blueprint that defines the properties and behaviors of an object. An **object** is an instance of a class, containing specific values for the properties defined in the class. In Unity, classes often represent entities in the game, such as players, enemies, and items, each with their own properties and behaviors.

Defining a Class

A class in C# is defined with the class keyword and typically contains fields, properties, methods, and constructors that define the data and behavior of the object it creates. Here's a simple example:

```csharp
csharp

public class Player
{
    public int health = 100;
    public int score = 0;

    public void TakeDamage(int damage)
    {
        health -= damage;
        Debug.Log("Player's health is now: " + health);
    }

    public void AddScore(int points)
    {
        score += points;
        Debug.Log("Player's score is now: " + score);
    }
}
```

This Player class has two fields (health and score) and two methods (TakeDamage() and AddScore()). It encapsulates the properties and behaviors of a player character.

Creating Objects from Classes

In Unity, you create objects by attaching scripts that define classes to GameObjects. Each GameObject with a script attached acts as an instance of that class, with its own set of values for properties like health and score.

Example of Creating an Object in Unity:

- Attach the Player script to a GameObject in the Unity Editor. Each GameObject with this script will have its own independent health and score values.

```
csharp

Player player = new Player();   // Instantiating a new Player
object
player.TakeDamage(10);          // Calls the TakeDamage method
```

Each GameObject with the Player class behaves according to the code within the class. In Unity, you typically rely on MonoBehaviour to work within the Unity environment, meaning scripts are created as components attached to GameObjects rather than instantiated manually.

Inheritance, Polymorphism, and Encapsulation Explained

OOP is defined by several advanced concepts that promote code reusability and flexibility. These include **inheritance**, **polymorphism**, and **encapsulation**, each playing a vital role in building complex game systems in Unity.

Inheritance

Inheritance allows you to create a base class with common functionality and have other classes (child classes) inherit from it, gaining access to its properties and methods. In Unity, this is particularly useful for creating general game elements, like a Character class, and then deriving specific classes like Player or Enemy.

Example of Inheritance:

- Let's create a base class Character with general properties like health and methods like Move(). We'll then create child classes, Player and Enemy, that inherit from Character.

```
csharp
```

```
public class Character
{
    public int health = 100;

    public virtual void TakeDamage(int damage)
    {
        health -= damage;
        Debug.Log("Character takes " + damage + " damage. Health:
        " + health);
    }
}

public class Player : Character
{
    public void Attack()
    {
        Debug.Log("Player attacks with weapon.");
    }
}

public class Enemy : Character
{
    public void Roar()
    {
        Debug.Log("Enemy roars menacingly.");
    }
}
```

Here:

- Player and Enemy inherit the health property and TakeDamage() method from Character.
- Player has an additional Attack() method, and Enemy has a Roar() method, adding unique functionality to each class.

Polymorphism

Polymorphism allows child classes to provide specific implementations of methods defined in a base class. Using polymorphism, you can call the same method on different objects and have each object respond differently based on its class type.

Using Polymorphism with virtual and override Keywords:

- In the example above, we could make TakeDamage() a virtual method in Character, allowing each child class to override it with a custom implementation.

```csharp
public class Character
{
    public int health = 100;

    public virtual void TakeDamage(int damage)
    {
        health -= damage;
        Debug.Log("Character takes " + damage + " damage. Health:
        " + health);
    }
}

public class Player : Character
{
    public override void TakeDamage(int damage)
    {
        health -= damage / 2; // Reduced damage due to armor
        Debug.Log("Player takes " + (damage / 2) + " damage.
        Health: " + health);
    }
}

public class Enemy : Character
{
    public override void TakeDamage(int damage)
    {
        health -= damage; // Full damage for enemies
```

```
Debug.Log("Enemy takes " + damage + " damage. Health: " +
health);
    }
}
```

- In this example, when TakeDamage() is called on a Player or Enemy instance, each object's unique version of TakeDamage() is executed.

Encapsulation

Encapsulation is the practice of hiding an object's internal data and controlling access through methods. In Unity, encapsulation is useful for managing object properties like health and score, providing controlled access through getter and setter methods.

Using Encapsulation for Health:

- By making the health field private, you ensure that it can only be modified through the TakeDamage() and Heal() methods, preventing accidental or unauthorized changes.

```csharp
csharp

public class Character
{
    private int health = 100;

    public void TakeDamage(int damage)
    {
        health -= damage;
        health = Mathf.Max(health, 0); // Ensures health doesn't
        drop below 0
        Debug.Log("Character's health is now: " + health);
    }
```

```
    public int GetHealth()
    {
        return health;
    }
}
```

In this setup:

- health is private, so other classes cannot modify it directly.
- Only TakeDamage() can reduce health, and GetHealth() provides read-only access.

Practical Application of OOP in Unity Scripts

Let's explore a more advanced example of applying these OOP principles to manage characters in a Unity game. We'll create a simple combat system where Player and Enemy characters interact using the principles of inheritance, polymorphism, and encapsulation.

Setting Up a Combat System with OOP

In this scenario, we'll create a Character base class with properties like health and methods for taking and dealing damage. Then, we'll define Player and Enemy subclasses with unique behaviors.

Create the Character Base Class:

- This class provides shared properties and methods.

```csharp
public class Character : MonoBehaviour
{
    protected int health = 100;
```

```
    public virtual void TakeDamage(int damage)
    {
        health -= damage;
        if (health <= 0)
        {
            Debug.Log("Character has been defeated.");
        }
        else
        {
            Debug.Log("Character's health is now: " + health);
        }
    }

    public void Heal(int amount)
    {
        health += amount;
        Debug.Log("Character healed. Health is now: " + health);
    }
}
```

Define the Player and Enemy Subclasses:

- The Player and Enemy classes override TakeDamage() and add unique methods.

```
csharp

public class Player : Character
{
    public override void TakeDamage(int damage)
    {
        health -= damage / 2; // Player takes half damage
        Debug.Log("Player takes " + (damage / 2) + " damage.
        Health: " + health);
    }
```

```
    public void Attack(Enemy enemy)
    {
        Debug.Log("Player attacks enemy!");
        enemy.TakeDamage(20);
    }
}

public class Enemy : Character
{
    public override void TakeDamage(int damage)
    {
        health -= damage; // Enemy takes full damage
        Debug.Log("Enemy takes " + damage + " damage. Health: " +
        health);
    }

    public void Roar()
    {
        Debug.Log("Enemy roars!");
    }
}
```

Implementing the Combat System in Unity:

- Attach the Player and Enemy scripts to GameObjects in your Unity scene. To simulate combat, create a script to call methods between the player and enemy.

```csharp
public class CombatManager : MonoBehaviour
{
    public Player player;
    public Enemy enemy;

    void Start()
    {
```

```
        player.Attack(enemy); // Player attacks enemy, reducing
        health
        enemy.Roar();          // Enemy roars in response
    }
}
```

In this setup:

- player.Attack(enemy) calls the Attack method on the player, passing the enemy as a target.
- The enemy.TakeDamage(20) method adjusts the enemy's health based on the damage dealt, demonstrating inheritance and polymorphism.

Understanding and applying OOP concepts like classes and objects, inheritance, polymorphism, and encapsulation in Unity can drastically improve your game's code structure, readability, and maintainability. These principles help you model game elements more intuitively and build complex mechanics with reusable code. By mastering OOP, you're better equipped to create flexible and scalable systems, making your games more organized and easier to expand upon as they grow in complexity.

Hands-On: Building a Basic Console Application in C#

Before jumping into Unity, it's helpful to build a simple console application in C# to understand the basics of the language without Unity's added complexity. A console application provides a command-line interface where you can see program outputs and user interactions directly, offering a clean environment to experiment with C# fundamentals like variables, control flow, and methods.

In this hands-on section, we'll create a console application that asks for the user's name, greets them, and performs a basic calculation. This example will cover everything from setting up a new project in Visual Studio to writing, running, and testing C# code.

Setting Up Your Console Application in Visual Studio
Open Visual Studio:

- If you don't have Visual Studio installed, download it from the official Visual Studio website and choose the free Community edition.
- When installing, make sure to include the **.NET desktop development** workload, which provides the tools necessary for C# console applications.

Create a New Project:

- Open Visual Studio, select **Create a new project**.
- Choose **Console App (.NET Core)** from the list of templates. This setup creates a project that runs in a console window, ideal for learning C# fundamentals.
- Name your project (e.g., BasicConsoleApp), choose a location for saving it, and click **Create**.

Project Setup:

- Visual Studio will generate a basic Program.cs file with a Main method. This is the entry point of the application, where execution begins.

Writing Your First Console Application

Let's start by creating a simple console program that performs the following tasks:

Asks for the user's name.

Greets the user with their name.

Asks the user for two numbers, adds them together, and displays the result.

Step 1: Display a Welcome Message

In the Main method of Program.cs, add code to print a welcome message to the console:

```csharp
using System;

namespace BasicConsoleApp
{
    class Program
    {
        static void Main(string[] args)
        {
            Console.WriteLine("Welcome to the Basic Console
            Application!");
        }
    }
}
```

- Console.WriteLine is a method that outputs text to the console. In this example, it displays the welcome message.

Step 2: Ask for the User's Name

Next, let's ask the user for their name and store it in a variable.

```csharp
Console.Write("Enter your name: ");
string userName = Console.ReadLine();
Console.WriteLine("Hello, " + userName + "!");
```

- Console.Write displays text without moving to a new line.
- Console.ReadLine waits for the user to enter text and press Enter, then stores the input as a string in userName.
- Console.WriteLine then greets the user by appending userName to a

greeting message.

Step 3: Ask for Two Numbers and Perform a Calculation

Now, let's ask the user for two numbers, add them together, and display the result.

csharp

```
Console.Write("Enter the first number: ");
int number1 = Convert.ToInt32(Console.ReadLine());

Console.Write("Enter the second number: ");
int number2 = Convert.ToInt32(Console.ReadLine());

int sum = number1 + number2;
Console.WriteLine("The sum of " + number1 + " and " + number2 + "
is: " + sum);
```

- Console.ReadLine captures the user input as a string, and Convert.ToInt32 converts it into an integer (int).
- The sum variable stores the result of adding number1 and number2.
- Finally, Console.WriteLine displays the sum.

Full Code Example

Here's the complete code for the basic console application:

csharp

```
using System;

namespace BasicConsoleApp
{
    class Program
    {
        static void Main(string[] args)
```

```
    {
        Console.WriteLine("Welcome to the Basic Console
        Application!");

        // Get the user's name
        Console.Write("Enter your name: ");
        string userName = Console.ReadLine();
        Console.WriteLine("Hello, " + userName + "!");

        // Get two numbers from the user and calculate their
        sum
        Console.Write("Enter the first number: ");
        int number1 = Convert.ToInt32(Console.ReadLine());

        Console.Write("Enter the second number: ");
        int number2 = Convert.ToInt32(Console.ReadLine());

        int sum = number1 + number2;
        Console.WriteLine("The sum of " + number1 + " and " +
        number2 + " is: " + sum);
    }
  }
}
```

Running and Testing Your Console Application

To run the application in Visual Studio:

Click on the **Start** button (green arrow) or press F5.

The console window will open, displaying the welcome message and prompting you to enter your name and two numbers.

Sample Output:

```
mathematica


Welcome to the Basic Console Application!
Enter your name: Alice
Hello, Alice!
Enter the first number: 5
```

```
Enter the second number: 10
The sum of 5 and 10 is: 15
```

Exploring and Modifying the Application

Now that the basic application is working, let's explore how you can expand on it to experiment with more C# concepts.

1. Adding a Multiplication Option

Let's add a feature that multiplies two numbers if the user chooses to.

Add a prompt for the user to select an operation (addition or multiplication).

Use a conditional statement to execute the appropriate operation.

```csharp
Console.Write("Choose an operation (add/multiply): ");
string operation = Console.ReadLine();

if (operation == "add")
{
    int sum = number1 + number2;
    Console.WriteLine("The sum is: " + sum);
}
else if (operation == "multiply")
{
    int product = number1 * number2;
    Console.WriteLine("The product is: " + product);
}
else
{
    Console.WriteLine("Invalid operation selected.");
}
```

2. Using a Method to Perform Calculations

Refactor the code to use methods, improving organization and reusability.

csharp

```
// Method for addition
static int Add(int a, int b)
{
    return a + b;
}

// Method for multiplication
static int Multiply(int a, int b)
{
    return a * b;
}
```

Then, modify the main code to use these methods:

csharp

```
if (operation == "add")
{
    int result = Add(number1, number2);
    Console.WriteLine("The sum is: " + result);
}
else if (operation == "multiply")
{
    int result = Multiply(number1, number2);
    Console.WriteLine("The product is: " + result);
}
```

This hands-on exercise demonstrates how to set up a console application in C# and use fundamental programming concepts such as input handling, variables, basic arithmetic, and control flow. Console applications are an excellent way to learn the basics of C# before applying these skills in Unity, where similar principles are used but with added complexity related to game objects and visuals.

Unity Basics and Your First Game

U nity is a popular game development engine that offers a user-friendly environment for creating interactive 2D and 3D experiences. To build a game in Unity, you must first set up and configure your project correctly, and then understand key Unity concepts like Scenes, GameObjects, and Components. This chapter will guide you through setting up your first Unity project, creating and configuring it in Unity Hub, and introduce you to essential Unity structures.

Setting Up Your First Unity Project

When starting a new project in Unity, setting it up properly can save you time and improve workflow efficiency. This setup phase involves understanding Unity Hub, selecting the right settings, and organizing your project files. Unity Hub is the management interface for creating and launching projects, installing Unity versions, and accessing learning resources.

Creating and Configuring a New Project in Unity Hub

Unity Hub simplifies managing multiple projects and versions of Unity, allowing you to control your development environment.

Step 1: Open Unity Hub

- **Download Unity Hub**: If you haven't already, download and install Unity Hub from Unity's official website.

- **Launch Unity Hub**: Open Unity Hub, where you'll find options for creating, managing, and accessing projects.

Step 2: Install a Unity Version

Unity Hub allows you to install and manage multiple versions of Unity, which is especially helpful when working on projects that require specific versions.

Go to the Installs Tab: Select the **Installs** tab in Unity Hub to view or add Unity versions.

Add a New Version: Click **Add**, choose the latest Long-Term Support (LTS) version (recommended for stability), and select any additional components you might need (e.g., Android or iOS Build Support if targeting mobile platforms).

Manage Versions: All installed versions will appear under the **Installs** tab, allowing you to update, remove, or switch between them as needed.

Step 3: Create a New Project

Navigate to the Projects Tab: Go to the **Projects** tab in Unity Hub, where you can create a new project by clicking **New Project**.

Choose a Template:

- **3D Core**: Ideal for developing 3D games with Unity's standard rendering pipeline.
- **2D Core**: Optimized for 2D game development, pre-configured with tools for sprite management and 2D physics.
- **Universal Render Pipeline (URP)**: Supports optimized graphics across multiple platforms, suitable for high-quality visuals on mobile, desktop, and console.
- **High Definition Render Pipeline (HDRP)**: Best for high-fidelity graphics in projects targeting powerful PCs or consoles.
- **VR or AR Templates**: Available for immersive applications, offering preconfigured settings for VR and AR hardware.

Set Project Details:

- **Name**: Choose a clear and descriptive name, such as FirstUnityGame, to identify your project.
- **Location**: Select a folder where Unity will save the project files.
- **Organization**: If working with Unity Teams or a company, you can specify an organization here.

Create the Project: Click **Create Project**. Unity Hub will launch Unity Editor, and your new project will open in a fresh window.

Understanding Scenes, GameObjects, and Components

Unity uses a component-based architecture, where all gameplay elements are composed of GameObjects and Components within Scenes. These concepts are central to Unity's framework and understanding them is essential for building any game in Unity.

Scenes: Organizing Your Game's Structure

A **Scene** in Unity is a container for all objects, settings, and components that make up a particular game level, environment, or interface. Scenes allow you to organize your game into separate spaces, making it easier to manage complex projects by dividing them into parts.

What is a Scene?:

- A Scene contains everything within a particular section of the game, from environments and characters to UI elements and audio sources.
- Each Scene is represented as a .unity file and can be accessed, loaded, or saved from Unity's **Hierarchy** and **Scene** views.

Working with Scenes:

- Unity automatically creates a default Scene when a new project is initialized. To create additional Scenes, go to **File > New Scene** or use **Ctrl + N**.

- Save your Scene by selecting **File > Save As** and naming it something relevant like MainScene or Level1.
- **Scene Management**: You can load, switch, and control Scenes programmatically, allowing you to move between levels or load different areas based on gameplay requirements.

Hierarchy and Inspector Windows:

- **Hierarchy Window**: Displays all GameObjects within the current Scene in a tree structure. You can parent GameObjects to each other here, creating organized structures and controlling groups of objects more easily.
- **Inspector Window**: Displays the selected object's properties, allowing you to view and adjust settings for each GameObject and its Components.

GameObjects: Core Building Blocks in Unity

A **GameObject** is the fundamental element in Unity, serving as a container for Components that define its properties, appearance, and behavior. Each GameObject represents an object within your Scene, from a player character to environmental elements like trees or buildings.

Creating GameObjects:

- You can create a GameObject by going to **GameObject > Create Empty** or by selecting one of the preconfigured objects under **3D Object** (e.g., Cube, Sphere) or **2D Object** (e.g., Sprite).
- **Empty GameObjects** are often used as organizational containers, grouping other GameObjects to manage them collectively.

The Transform Component:

- Every GameObject has a **Transform** component, which defines its position, rotation, and scale in the Scene. Transform is the default component and cannot be removed.

- Use the Transform component to arrange and organize GameObjects within your Scene, adjusting coordinates, angles, and size.

Hierarchy and Parenting:

- Unity's Hierarchy lets you parent GameObjects to create structures where child objects inherit transformations from their parent. For example, a Player GameObject can act as a parent to components like Head, Arms, and Legs, which are child objects.
- Parenting simplifies the movement and scaling of related objects, as adjusting the parent's Transform affects all child objects.

Components: Defining GameObject Behavior and Properties

Components are modular elements that add specific functionality to GameObjects. Unity's component-based system allows you to mix and match different Components to create complex behaviors without writing custom code for each behavior.

Core Components in Unity:

- **Transform**: Defines the position, rotation, and scale of the GameObject. Every GameObject has a Transform component by default.
- **Renderer**: Controls how an object is visually displayed. For 3D objects, use a **Mesh Renderer**, and for 2D objects, use a **Sprite Renderer**.
- **Collider**: Provides a shape for detecting collisions, such as **Box Collider**, **Sphere Collider**, or **Mesh Collider**. Colliders are essential for interactions like player collisions with walls or objects.
- **Rigidbody**: Enables physics interactions for the GameObject, allowing it to respond to gravity, collisions, and forces. This component is crucial for dynamic objects that need realistic physics, like a ball rolling down a hill.
- **Scripts**: Custom scripts written in C# let you define specific behaviors for GameObjects, such as player movement, score tracking, or enemy

AI.

Adding Components to GameObjects:

- Select a GameObject in the **Hierarchy** or **Scene** view, then click **Add Component** in the **Inspector** window to attach a new component.
- Each component has unique settings. For example, in the Rigidbody component, you can adjust properties like **Mass** and **Drag** to modify how it interacts with the physics system.
- Stacking components allows you to create complex interactions. For instance, a player GameObject might have a Rigidbody for physics, a Collider for collisions, a Script for player control, and a Renderer to display the character model.

Example: Creating a Basic GameObject with Components
Let's walk through creating a simple player GameObject that can interact with the environment:
Create a Player GameObject:

- Go to **GameObject > 3D Object > Capsule** to add a Capsule to the Scene, which we'll use as the player character.
- Rename the Capsule Player in the Hierarchy for clarity.

Add Components:

- **Rigidbody**: Select Player in the Hierarchy, go to the Inspector, and click **Add Component**. Search for **Rigidbody** and add it. The Rigidbody allows the player to interact with Unity's physics engine, including gravity.
- **Collider**: By default, the Capsule has a **Capsule Collider**, which defines the player's shape for collision detection. You can adjust the size and offset if needed.
- **Script for Player Control**: Go to **Add Component > New Script**,

81

name it PlayerController, and open it in Visual Studio to write custom code for player movement (e.g., moving forward, backward, or jumping).

Organize GameObjects in the Hierarchy:

- You can add Empty GameObjects to the Scene and parent objects to them for better organization. For instance, create an empty GameObject called Environment and add objects like Ground and Obstacles as its children to keep your Scene organized.

Understanding Scenes, GameObjects, and Components is essential for building and organizing any Unity project. These elements form the backbone of Unity's structure, allowing you to create interactive, complex environments in a manageable way. Scenes organize your game into discrete levels or areas, GameObjects represent everything within those Scenes, and Components bring GameObjects to life by defining their properties and behavior.

Importing and Managing Assets

In Unity, assets are the building blocks that make up your game's environment, characters, sounds, and more. Managing these assets effectively is essential for keeping your project organized, improving workflow, and minimizing file size. Unity offers tools like the **Asset Store** to source assets, and you can also import your own. This section provides an in-depth guide on using the Asset Store and best practices for organizing assets in Unity.

Introduction to Unity's Asset Store

The Unity Asset Store is a marketplace where developers can find free and paid assets, from 3D models and textures to sounds and scripts, designed to speed up development. The Asset Store provides high-quality assets that you can import directly into your project, saving you time and effort. It's a great starting point for beginners, as it offers essential resources for prototyping and experimentation.

Accessing the Asset Store

Open Unity and go to **Window > Asset Store**. This will open the Asset Store window directly within the Unity Editor.

Browse and Search: You can search for specific assets using the search bar, or browse by categories like 3D Models, Textures, Audio, Tools, and Scripts.

Account Sign-In: You need a Unity account to download assets from the store. If you don't have one, you can create an account for free at Unity's website.

Finding Suitable Assets

When searching for assets, consider factors like quality, compatibility, and licensing.

- **Compatibility**: Check the Unity version compatibility listed on the asset page to ensure it works with your project.
- **Quality**: Assets on the store have user ratings, reviews, and previews, which can help assess the quality and functionality.
- **Licensing**: Most assets are free for personal use but may have restrictions on commercial use. Review the asset's license to ensure it aligns with your project needs.

Importing Assets from the Asset Store
Download and Import:

- After selecting an asset, click **Download** (or **Buy** for paid assets). Once downloaded, the button will change to **Import**.
- Click **Import** to bring the asset into your project. A dialog box will appear, allowing you to select which files to import.

Select Specific Files:

- Review the asset package contents and select only the files you need. For example, you may choose to import only textures or 3D models, leaving out unnecessary scripts or extras.
- Click **Import** to finalize, and the files will appear in your **Assets** folder.

Best Practices for Organizing Assets in Unity

Efficient asset organization is crucial, particularly in larger projects where a large number of files can become overwhelming. A well-structured asset library simplifies asset management, reduces errors, and optimizes the overall workflow.

1. Use a Standard Folder Structure

Unity doesn't impose a folder structure, so it's helpful to create a standardized structure to categorize different asset types.

A typical project structure might look like this:

- **Assets**: The main folder containing all project files.
- **Art**: Visual elements, including textures, sprites, and models.
- **Textures**: Stores texture files (e.g., .png, .jpg).
- **Materials**: Holds material files that define how textures appear on models.
- **Audio**: Sound effects, background music, and voiceover files.
- **Prefabs**: Reusable GameObjects with preset configurations.
- **Scenes**: Stores Unity Scene files that define game levels, menus, and other game areas.
- **Scripts**: Houses custom scripts, organized by functionality (e.g., Player, Enemy, UI).
- **Animations**: Contains animation files and Animator controllers.
- **UI**: User interface assets, such as images, buttons, and fonts.

This folder structure keeps assets categorized, making it easier to find and modify specific files.

2. Use Clear Naming Conventions

Using descriptive names makes assets easy to find and prevents confusion. Create a consistent naming convention that includes prefixes to identify asset types or purposes. For example:

- **Textures**: T_GrassTexture, T_CharacterSkin
- **Materials**: M_Wood, M_Metal
- **Scripts**: PlayerController, EnemyAI
- **Audio**: SFX_Explosion, BGM_Level1

This naming system allows you to identify asset types quickly, even in a large project.

3. Group Third-Party Assets in Separate Folders

When importing third-party assets from the Asset Store, keep them organized in a separate folder, such as Assets > ThirdParty > AssetName. This prevents your main project structure from becoming cluttered and makes it easy to locate, update, or remove third-party assets if needed.

4. Use Prefabs for Reusable GameObjects

Prefabs are one of Unity's most powerful tools, allowing you to create reusable GameObjects with pre-configured components and settings. For instance, you might create a **Player** prefab that includes the player model, Collider, Rigidbody, and control scripts.

- **Benefits of Prefabs**: Prefabs allow for easy updating of multiple instances across the project. When you make changes to a prefab, all instances of that prefab will automatically update.
- **Prefab Organization**: Store prefabs in a dedicated folder like Assets > Prefabs, and create subfolders if necessary (e.g., Prefabs > Characters, Prefabs > Environment).

5. Regularly Clean Up Unused Assets

Unused assets can clutter your project and increase file size, affecting performance and making it harder to locate active files. To keep your project optimized:

Identify Unused Assets: Unity doesn't automatically highlight unused assets, but tools like **Unity's Asset Cleaner** can help. Alternatively, you can manually remove assets by checking for references.

Delete or Archive: Remove or archive unused assets regularly, especially before publishing or sharing your project.

6. Label and Tag Assets for Easy Searching

Unity allows you to tag and label assets, which makes it easier to search and filter files in large projects. Labels can be especially helpful when working with assets that share similar file types or functions.

- **Adding Labels**: Right-click an asset, select **Labels > Add Label**, and create relevant tags like Environment, Character, or UI.
- **Using Labels in Search**: In the Project window, type the label name in the search bar to filter assets with that label.

7. Backup and Version Control

For collaborative projects or those with extensive assets, version control is crucial. Using a system like Git, Unity Collaborate, or a cloud storage backup allows you to track asset changes, revert to previous versions, and protect your project from data loss.

- **Git**: Platforms like GitHub, GitLab, or Bitbucket are popular for version control and work well with Unity.
- **Unity Collaborate**: Unity's built-in version control system is accessible for teams and offers cloud storage for easy collaboration.

Example: Importing, Organizing, and Using Assets from the Asset Store

To illustrate the import and organization process, let's go through an example of downloading a 3D model asset from the Unity Asset Store and integrating it into your project.

Open the Asset Store:

- In Unity, go to **Window > Asset Store** and search for a free asset, like "tree model."

Download and Import:

- Click **Download**, and once finished, click **Import**. Unity will display a dialog showing the asset's contents.
- Review the contents and select only the files you need. For instance, if you only need the model and textures, uncheck other assets like scripts or animations.

Organize the Imported Files:

- After import, place the assets in a designated folder. For example, move the tree model files to Assets > Models > Environment.
- If the asset includes textures and materials, place them in Assets > Textures > Environment and Assets > Materials > Environment folders for better organization.

Convert the Asset to a Prefab:

- Drag the tree model from the Project window to the Scene to create a GameObject.
- Add any components you need, like a Collider for physics interactions.
- Finally, drag the configured GameObject from the Scene back into the **Prefabs** folder to create a prefab. This prefab can now be reused across your game levels.

Effective asset management in Unity is essential for efficient game development. Unity's Asset Store offers a vast collection of resources, allowing you to import ready-made assets that speed up your workflow. Once assets are in your project, organizing them using a standardized folder structure, clear naming conventions, and prefabs will keep your project streamlined and easy to navigate.

Building Your First Simple 2D Game

Creating a simple 2D game is an excellent way to apply Unity fundamentals, including setting up a scene, moving GameObjects, and adding player interaction. This section will guide you through setting up the game scene, writing scripts for movement, and implementing basic player controls to bring your game to life.

Setting Up the Game Scene: Adding Background and GameObjects

A game scene serves as a container where you position and manage all the elements that make up a game level or environment. Here, we'll add a background and key objects, such as a player character and collectible items, to set up the scene.

Step 1: Setting Up the Scene
Create a New Scene:

- In Unity, go to **File > New Scene** to create a fresh scene.
- Save the scene by selecting **File > Save As** and naming it something like Simple2DGame.

Switch to 2D Mode:

- Ensure the Scene view is set to **2D** (at the top of the Scene window). This view helps visualize the layout, as we're working on a flat plane.

Step 2: Adding a Background
Import a Background Image:

- Import a 2D image for your background by dragging it from your file system into Unity's **Assets** folder.
- Once imported, drag the background image into the **Hierarchy** window to add it to the Scene.

Position the Background:

- Use the **Rect Tool** (shortcut T) to scale and position the background, ensuring it covers the camera view.

Layering the Background:

- In the Inspector, set the **Order in Layer** of the background to a low value (e.g., -1) so it remains behind other GameObjects.

Step 3: Adding Main GameObjects
Add the primary interactive elements to the scene, including a player character and collectible items.
Create the Player Character:

- Import or create a 2D sprite for the player, like a character or object icon.
- Drag the sprite into the Scene, which creates a new GameObject in the Hierarchy. Rename this GameObject to Player.

Add Collectibles:

- Import a sprite for collectibles (like a coin or star) and drag it into the Scene to create a collectible GameObject.
- Duplicate this GameObject (Ctrl + D or **Cmd + D**) to create multiple

collectibles and arrange them around the player.

Organize GameObjects:

- Name each collectible for clarity (e.g., Coin1, Coin2), and group them in the Hierarchy under an empty GameObject named Collectibles to keep the Hierarchy organized.

Basic Scripting in Unity: Moving GameObjects

To allow player movement, we'll create a script that enables the player to move using keyboard inputs. Unity uses C# scripting for custom behaviors, and this section will cover how to set up a movement script.

Creating a Player Movement Script
Create the Script:

- In the **Assets** folder, right-click, select **Create > C# Script**, and name it PlayerMovement.
- Open the script by double-clicking to edit it in Visual Studio or your preferred C# editor.

Writing the Movement Code

In this script, we'll use Unity's Update() method to capture player input and apply movement.

```csharp
using UnityEngine;

public class PlayerMovement : MonoBehaviour
{
    public float speed = 5.0f;

    void Update()
    {
```

```
    // Capture player input
    float horizontalInput = Input.GetAxis("Horizontal");
    float verticalInput = Input.GetAxis("Vertical");

    // Calculate movement direction and apply speed
    Vector3 movement = new Vector3(horizontalInput,
    verticalInput, 0) * speed * Time.deltaTime;
    transform.position += movement;
  }
}
```

Explanation of the Script:

- **Input.GetAxis**: Input.GetAxis("Horizontal") and Input.GetAxis("Vertical") capture input values ranging from -1 to 1 based on arrow or WASD key presses.
- **Vector3**: movement defines the direction and magnitude of movement based on input and speed.
- **transform.position**: Updates the player's position by adding the movement vector each frame.

Attach the Script to the Player:

- Save the script, return to Unity, and attach PlayerMovement to the Player GameObject by dragging it to the Player or clicking **Add Component** in the Inspector.

Testing Movement:

- Press **Play** to test the player movement. You should be able to move the player around with the arrow keys or WASD keys.

Adding User Interaction and Basic Controls

To make the game more interactive, we'll implement collision detection to allow the player to collect items. We'll also add a scoring system to display the player's progress.

Step 1: Adding a Score System

Create a UI Text Element:

- In the Hierarchy, go to **GameObject > UI > Text** to add a text element.
- Rename it ScoreText and position it in the top corner of the screen.
- Customize the font size, color, and alignment in the Inspector, and set the initial text to "Score: 0".

Create a ScoreManager Script:

- Create a new script called ScoreManager in the Scripts folder.
- Open the script and add the following code to manage the player's score:

```csharp
using UnityEngine;
using UnityEngine.UI;

public class ScoreManager : MonoBehaviour
{
    public Text scoreText;
    private int score = 0;

    public void AddScore(int value)
    {
        score += value;
        scoreText.text = "Score: " + score;
    }
}
```

Explanation of the Script:

- **AddScore()**: Adds points to score and updates scoreText.

- **scoreText**: References the UI text that displays the score in the game.

Attach the ScoreManager:

- Attach ScoreManager to an empty GameObject called GameManager in the Hierarchy.
- Drag ScoreText from the Hierarchy to the scoreText field in ScoreManager's Inspector to link the UI element.

Step 2: Detecting Collisions with Collectibles

Add collision detection so the player can collect items and increase their score.

Add Colliders:

- Ensure the Player and each collectible have **Collider2D** components. Use **Circle Collider 2D** or **Box Collider 2D** for simple shapes.
- Enable **Is Trigger** on the collectibles' colliders, so they don't physically block the player.

Create a Collectible Script:

- Create a new script named Collectible.
- Open it and add code to detect player interactions:

```csharp
using UnityEngine;

public class Collectible : MonoBehaviour
{
    public int scoreValue = 10;

    void OnTriggerEnter2D(Collider2D other)
```

```
    {
        if (other.CompareTag("Player"))
        {
            ScoreManager scoreManager =
            FindObjectOfType<ScoreManager>();
            scoreManager.AddScore(scoreValue);
            Destroy(gameObject);
        }
    }
}
```

Explanation of the Script:

- **OnTriggerEnter2D**: Detects when another object (in this case, the Player) enters the collectible's trigger area.
- **scoreValue**: Defines how many points the collectible is worth. When the player collides, it adds scoreValue to the total score.
- **Destroy(gameObject)**: Removes the collectible from the scene after collection.

Tagging the Player:

- Select the Player in the Hierarchy, go to the Inspector, and assign it the **Player** tag. This lets the Collectible script identify it during collision events.

Testing the Game:

- Press **Play** to test. When the player touches a collectible, it should disappear, and the score should update accordingly.

In this guide, you created a basic 2D game in Unity by setting up a scene, adding movement with a custom script, and implementing interaction between the player and collectible items. These skills—scene setup, object movement, and collision handling—are essential to building interactive gameplay in Unity. By experimenting further, you can add complexity, such as more sophisticated player controls or different types of collectibles, to expand your game's mechanics and enhance the player experience.

Mini Project: Making a Basic 2D Clicker Game

A clicker game, sometimes called an idle game, is a genre that involves repetitive player actions, often clicking, to earn in-game currency or rewards. Creating a basic 2D clicker game in Unity is an ideal project to learn about UI elements, scripting, and incrementing values based on player actions. This project will guide you through setting up a simple clicker game where the player clicks on an object to earn points and can spend those points to unlock rewards or upgrades.

Project Overview

In this clicker game, players will:
Click on an on-screen object to gain points.
See their score update in real-time.
Purchase upgrades to increase the points earned per click.

Setting Up the Game Scene
Step 1: Create a New Scene and Basic Layout
Create a New Scene:

- Go to **File > New Scene** in Unity, then save it as ClickerGame.

Switch to 2D Mode:

- In the Scene view, make sure **2D** mode is active for a clear, top-down perspective on your 2D assets.

Step 2: Setting Up the Game Object for Clicking
Create a Clickable Object:

- Import or create a simple 2D sprite (e.g., a circle, coin, or star) to represent the object players will click.
- Drag the sprite from the **Assets** folder into the **Hierarchy** to add it to the Scene.
- Rename this GameObject to ClickableObject for clarity.

Position and Scale the Object:

- Use the **Rect Tool** to adjust the size and position of the object so it's easily clickable at the center of the screen.

Add Collider2D:

- Attach a **Collider2D** component to the ClickableObject (e.g., **Circle Collider 2D** if it's a circular object) to detect clicks on it.
- Ensure **Is Trigger** is enabled to handle click events without physical interaction.

Adding the UI Elements for Score Display and Upgrades
Step 1: Set Up the Score Display
Add a Text Element:

- In the Hierarchy, go to **GameObject > UI > Text** to create a UI Text element.
- Rename it ScoreText and position it at the top of the screen. Adjust font size, color, and alignment in the Inspector.
- Set the initial text to "Score: 0".

Add Another Text for Upgrade Information:

- Duplicate ScoreText (Ctrl + D or Cmd + D) and rename it UpgradeInfo.
- Adjust its position below ScoreText, and set it to display upgrade information like "Click Power: 1".

Writing Scripts for Click Mechanics and Scoring

Step 1: Create a Game Manager Script

The **GameManager** script will handle the main gameplay logic, including score tracking, click detection, and upgrades.

Create the GameManager Script:

- In the **Scripts** folder, right-click, select **Create > C# Script**, and name it GameManager.
- Attach this script to an empty GameObject called GameManager in the Hierarchy.

Write the Code for the GameManager

Open GameManager.cs and add the following code:

```csharp
using UnityEngine;
using UnityEngine.UI;

public class GameManager : MonoBehaviour
{
    public Text scoreText;
    public Text upgradeInfoText;
    private int score = 0;
    private int clickPower = 1;
    private int upgradeCost = 10;

    void Start()
    {
        UpdateUI();
    }
}
```

```
public void OnObjectClicked()
{
    score += clickPower;
    UpdateUI();
}

public void UpgradeClickPower()
{
    if (score >= upgradeCost)
    {
        score -= upgradeCost;
        clickPower++;
        upgradeCost *= 2;
        UpdateUI();
    }
}

private void UpdateUI()
{
    scoreText.text = "Score: " + score;
    upgradeInfoText.text = "Click Power: " + clickPower +
    "\nUpgrade Cost: " + upgradeCost;
}
}
```

Explanation of the Script:

- **score**: Tracks the player's total score.
- **clickPower**: The number of points added per click.
- **upgradeCost**: The cost to upgrade click power.
- **OnObjectClicked()**: Adds points based on the current clickPower each time the player clicks the object.
- **UpgradeClickPower()**: Allows the player to spend points to increase clickPower.
- **UpdateUI()**: Updates ScoreText and UpgradeInfoText with the current values.

Link UI Elements:

- In the Inspector, assign ScoreText and UpgradeInfoText to their respective fields in the GameManager component.

Step 2: Detecting Clicks on the Object

Create a ClickableObject Script

The **ClickableObject** script will handle detecting clicks on the GameObject and then notifying the GameManager.

Create the Script:

- In the **Scripts** folder, create a new script named ClickableObject.
- Attach ClickableObject to the ClickableObject GameObject in the Hierarchy.

Write the Code for ClickableObject

Open ClickableObject.cs and add the following code:

```csharp
using UnityEngine;

public class ClickableObject : MonoBehaviour
{
    private GameManager gameManager;

    void Start()
    {
        gameManager = FindObjectOfType<GameManager>();
    }

    void OnMouseDown()
    {
        gameManager.OnObjectClicked();
    }
}
```

Explanation of the Script:

- **OnMouseDown()**: Unity calls this method when the player clicks on the GameObject's Collider. It then calls OnObjectClicked() in GameManager to increase the score.

Adding an Upgrade Button for Click Power

To let players purchase upgrades to increase their click power, we'll add a button to the UI.

Add a Button UI Element:

- In the Hierarchy, go to **GameObject > UI > Button** and rename it UpgradeButton.
- Move it near the bottom of the screen.

Configure the Button Text:

- Click the **Text** child of UpgradeButton in the Hierarchy and rename it to "Upgrade Click Power".

Link the Button to the Upgrade Function:

- Select UpgradeButton and in the Inspector, scroll to the **On Click ()** section.
- Click + to add a new OnClick event, drag the GameManager object into the event's field, and select GameManager > UpgradeClickPower.

Testing and Adjusting Game Balance

Step 1: Testing the Game

Press Play: Enter Play mode and test the clicker game by clicking the ClickableObject.

Check Score Updates: Confirm that each click increments the score by the clickPower value.

Upgrade Button: Click **Upgrade Click Power** once you have enough points. Ensure the score decreases by the upgradeCost and clickPower increases as expected.

Step 2: Adjusting Game Balance

- **Initial Click Power**: Adjust the initial value of clickPower if the game is too easy or difficult.
- **Upgrade Cost Scaling**: Modify upgradeCost *= 2 in UpgradeClickPower() to change how quickly upgrade prices increase, depending on your game's difficulty balance.

Expanding the Clicker Game

This basic structure can be expanded to add more depth and complexity:

- **Passive Income**: Introduce passive income, where players earn points over time without clicking.
- **Different Clickable Objects**: Add multiple clickable objects with varying point values or effects.
- **Additional Upgrades**: Introduce upgrades that increase passive income or offer multipliers on click power.

This 2D clicker game project introduces essential Unity concepts such as scripting, UI management, click detection, and incremental value changes. By following these steps, you've created a simple yet engaging clicker game that can be expanded and customized. This project provides a foundation for further exploration of UI, scripting, and gameplay mechanics in Unity.

Diving Deeper into Unity's 2D Capabilities

Unity offers robust tools for working with 2D elements, especially when it comes to using sprites and animations. In this chapter, we'll explore how to work with sprites and sprite sheets, and create animations to bring your 2D characters and elements to life. These techniques are fundamental for building engaging, visually dynamic 2D games.

Sprites and Animations

In Unity, **sprites** are 2D images used to represent characters, items, or backgrounds. **Animations** bring these sprites to life, adding movement and interaction. Unity's animation tools allow you to animate sprite-based characters and objects in various ways, from simple loops to complex, dynamic sequences.

What is a Sprite?

A sprite is a 2D graphic object that represents an individual visual asset in your game. Sprites can be static images or frames from a sprite sheet, and they're commonly used for characters, objects, backgrounds, and UI elements in 2D games.

Importing Sprites:

- To use a sprite, first import a 2D image into Unity by dragging it from your file system to the **Assets** folder.

- In the Inspector, set the **Texture Type** to **Sprite (2D and UI)** to ensure Unity recognizes it as a sprite.

Sprite Renderer:

- Attach a **Sprite Renderer** component to a GameObject to display the sprite in the game world. This component controls how the sprite appears, including its color, layer, and sorting order.

Sprite Sheet:

- A **sprite sheet** is a single image containing multiple frames of a sprite, arranged in a grid or sequence. Sprite sheets are particularly useful for animations, as each frame represents a different pose or movement stage.

Working with Sprites and Sprite Sheets

Using sprite sheets in Unity is an efficient way to handle character animations and multi-frame sequences. A sprite sheet groups all frames of an animation into one image file, which can be split in Unity to create individual frames for animations.

Step 1: Importing a Sprite Sheet
Import the Sprite Sheet:

- Drag a sprite sheet image into Unity's **Assets** folder. This image should contain all animation frames, arranged in a grid.

Set the Texture Type to Sprite (2D and UI):

- Select the sprite sheet in the Assets folder, go to the **Inspector**, and set **Texture Type** to **Sprite (2D and UI)**.
- Set **Sprite Mode** to **Multiple**. This setting lets you split the sprite sheet

into multiple frames.

Sprite Editor:

- With the sprite sheet selected, click **Sprite Editor** in the Inspector. Unity will open a new window, allowing you to slice the sprite sheet into individual sprites.

Slicing the Sprite Sheet:

- In the Sprite Editor, click **Slice** and choose the **Grid By Cell Size** or **Grid By Cell Count** option, depending on your sprite sheet's layout.
- Set the cell size or count to match the size of each individual sprite in the sheet.
- Click **Slice** to split the sheet into separate sprites, which Unity will treat as individual images.

Apply and Save:

- After slicing, click **Apply** in the Sprite Editor. Unity saves each frame as an individual sprite, accessible in the **Project** window.

Step 2: Organizing and Using Sprites from a Sprite Sheet
Naming Sprites:

- Unity automatically names sliced sprites based on the main sprite sheet's name. Rename them if necessary for easier identification, especially if you'll use them in different animations.

Creating Animation Frames:

- To create animations, select all frames for a particular animation sequence (e.g., Idle_1, Idle_2, Idle_3) and drag them into the **Scene** or **Hierarchy** view.

- Unity automatically generates an animation clip with the selected frames.

Using Sprites in the Scene:

- Drag individual sprites onto GameObjects in the Scene or Hierarchy to display static images, or use a sequence to create animations.

Creating and Using 2D Animations in Unity

Unity's **Animator** system allows you to create and control complex animations for your 2D sprites. With the **Animation** window, you can add keyframes, adjust timings, and combine multiple animation clips to create smooth, dynamic character animations.

Step 1: Creating an Animation Clip

An animation clip is a sequence of frames that play in order to animate a character or object.

Select the Sprite:

- In the **Project** window, select the sliced sprite frames you want to use for an animation, such as Idle or Walk frames.

Create an Animation Clip:

- Drag the selected frames onto the **Scene** view or Hierarchy. Unity prompts you to create a new animation clip.
- Name the animation clip (e.g., Idle, Walk, or Jump) and save it in a designated **Animations** folder in your Assets.

Customize the Animation Clip:

- Open the **Animation** window (Window > Animation > Animation) to adjust the timing of each frame.

- Modify the playback speed by adjusting the **Samples** value at the top of the Animation window. Lower values make the animation slower, while higher values make it faster.
- Reorder frames if needed to refine the animation sequence.

Step 2: Using the Animator Controller

The **Animator Controller** manages multiple animation clips and transitions, allowing you to define which animations play based on player inputs, conditions, or events.

Create an Animator Controller:

- In the **Assets** folder, right-click, select **Create > Animator Controller**, and name it (e.g., PlayerAnimator).
- Attach this Animator Controller to the GameObject with the Sprite Renderer, typically your player character.

Open the Animator Window:

- With the Animator Controller selected, open the **Animator** window (Window > Animation > Animator) to view and edit the animation state machine.
- In the Animator window, you'll see an **Entry** state connected to the default animation clip. Drag additional animation clips from the Project window into the Animator to add more states.

Setting Up Transitions:

- To create smooth transitions between animations (e.g., Idle to Walk), right-click an animation clip in the Animator window and select **Make Transition**.
- Drag from the current animation state to the target animation state to create a transition arrow.

- Select the transition, and in the **Inspector**, adjust **Conditions** to control when the transition occurs. For example, you might set a Speed parameter that determines if the player is moving (triggering Walk) or stationary (triggering Idle).

Step 3: Controlling Animations with Parameters and Scripts

Unity's Animator Controller uses parameters to determine which animations play based on game conditions or player input.

Adding Parameters:

- In the Animator window, go to the **Parameters** tab and add parameters such as Speed or IsJumping.
- **Float** parameters are useful for controlling animations based on movement speed, while **Bool** parameters can trigger specific actions, like jumping or attacking.

Using Scripts to Update Parameters

Write a script to update Animator parameters based on player input or gameplay events.

```csharp
using UnityEngine;

public class PlayerController : MonoBehaviour
{
    private Animator animator;
    private float speed;

    void Start()
    {
        animator = GetComponent<Animator>();
    }

    void Update()
```

```
    {
        // Capture player input
        float horizontalInput = Input.GetAxis("Horizontal");
        speed = Mathf.Abs(horizontalInput);

        // Update animator parameter
        animator.SetFloat("Speed", speed);

        // Handle movement
        transform.Translate(new Vector2(horizontalInput, 0) *
        Time.deltaTime);
    }
}
```

Explanation of the Script:

- **SetFloat("Speed", speed)**: Updates the Animator's Speed parameter based on player input.
- **Speed Parameter**: When Speed is greater than zero, the Walk animation plays. When zero, it transitions to Idle.

Step 4: Testing and Refining the Animation

- **Testing Transitions**: Enter Play mode and test the animations by moving the player character. Observe transitions between Idle and Walk.
- **Adjusting Transition Conditions**: Refine transition conditions in the Animator to make animations smoother. Modify **Exit Time** and **Transition Duration** for seamless transitions.

Working with sprites and animations is fundamental in 2D game development. By mastering sprite sheets, the Animator system, and animation control through scripts, you can create smooth and engaging character movements. This foundation allows you to expand into more complex animations, such as attack, jump, or special abilities, making your 2D games feel dynamic and responsive.

2D Physics and Collisions

Unity's 2D physics system enables developers to simulate real-world physical behaviors like gravity, collisions, and momentum in a 2D space. Understanding how to use **Rigidbodies** and **Colliders** is crucial for creating realistic and interactive 2D games. In this section, we'll explore how to set up Rigidbodies and Colliders and handle basic physics interactions and triggers.

Rigidbodies and Colliders Explained

Rigidbodies and **Colliders** are two fundamental components in Unity's physics engine, used to apply and detect forces and collisions for GameObjects. When working with 2D physics, it's essential to use **Rigidbody2D** and **Collider2D** components instead of their 3D counterparts to ensure compatibility with Unity's 2D physics engine.

Rigidbody2D: Applying Physics to GameObjects

A **Rigidbody2D** component allows a GameObject to be influenced by physical forces, such as gravity or collisions. Adding a Rigidbody2D enables the GameObject to respond dynamically to movement and interactions in the game environment.

Adding a Rigidbody2D Component:

- Select the GameObject (e.g., a player character or enemy) in the **Hierarchy**.
- In the **Inspector**, click **Add Component** and choose **Rigidbody2D**.

Rigidbody2D Properties:

- **Gravity Scale**: Controls the effect of gravity on the GameObject. Set to 1 by default, meaning it will fall as though under Earth's gravity. Setting it to 0 makes the object unaffected by gravity.

- **Mass**: Determines the object's weight, affecting how it interacts with forces and other objects.
- **Linear Drag and Angular Drag**: Influence how much the GameObject slows down over time. **Linear Drag** affects straight-line motion, while **Angular Drag** affects rotation.
- **Constraints**: Use **Freeze Position** and **Freeze Rotation** to prevent the object from moving or rotating on specific axes, useful in side-scrollers where rotation is often undesirable.

Collider2D: Detecting Collisions

A **Collider2D** component defines the shape of a GameObject for collision detection. Unity provides several types of 2D colliders, each suited to different shapes and use cases.

Types of Collider2D Components:

- **Box Collider 2D**: Ideal for rectangular or square objects, defining a box-shaped collision boundary.
- **Circle Collider 2D**: Best for circular or rounded objects.
- **Polygon Collider 2D**: Suitable for irregular shapes, allowing you to outline complex objects.
- **Edge Collider 2D**: Defines a boundary along a line, often used for terrain or platforms.
- **Composite Collider 2D**: Combines multiple colliders into one, improving efficiency for complex shapes.

Setting Up a Collider2D:

- Select the GameObject and go to **Add Component > Physics 2D**. Choose an appropriate Collider2D based on the object's shape.
- Adjust the collider's size and position in the Inspector to fit the GameObject accurately. Unity displays the collider as a green outline in the Scene view.

Is Trigger:

- Enabling **Is Trigger** on a Collider2D allows objects to pass through each other without a physical response (no collision force), but it still registers an interaction event. Triggers are useful for detecting interactions like pickups, hazards, or checkpoints without obstructing the player.

Handling Simple Physics Interactions and Triggers

Unity's physics interactions and triggers allow you to create dynamic and interactive elements in your game, such as jumping, picking up items, or triggering animations. Here, we'll explore setting up basic physics interactions and detecting triggers.

Step 1: Setting Up Basic Physics Interactions
Gravity and Movement:

- With a Rigidbody2D attached to your player character, it will fall due to gravity by default.
- To add movement, you can use player input and adjust the Rigidbody2D's velocity, enabling actions like running or jumping.

Applying Forces:

- Unity provides methods to apply physics-based forces, such as **AddForce()** and **velocity**.
- Use AddForce() to simulate physics-based motion, such as jumps or knockbacks.

Example: Applying an upward force for a jump.

```
csharp
```

```
public class PlayerController : MonoBehaviour
{
    private Rigidbody2D rb;
    public float jumpForce = 5f;

    void Start()
    {
        rb = GetComponent<Rigidbody2D>();
    }

    void Update()
    {
        if (Input.GetKeyDown(KeyCode.Space))
        {
            rb.AddForce(Vector2.up * jumpForce,
            ForceMode2D.Impulse);
        }
    }
}
```

- **Vector2.up** provides an upward direction, multiplied by the jumpForce to create a jumping effect.
- **ForceMode2D.Impulse** applies an instant force, perfect for jumps.

Bouncing and Friction:

- Adjust **Material** properties on Rigidbody2D to add effects like bounciness or friction.
- Go to **Assets > Create > Physics Material 2D** and create a new material. Set **Bounciness** and **Friction** values as desired, then apply it to the Rigidbody2D's **Material** field.

Step 2: Using Triggers for Interactions

Triggers enable you to detect when an object enters or exits an area without physical impact. This is ideal for pickups, checkpoints, or hazards.

Setting Up a Trigger:

- Attach a Collider2D to the GameObject, such as a coin or spike.
- In the Inspector, enable **Is Trigger** to make it a trigger collider.

Script for Trigger Detection

Add a script to the trigger object to detect when another collider enters it. In this example, we'll set up a coin that the player can collect.

```csharp
using UnityEngine;

public class Collectible : MonoBehaviour
{
    public int scoreValue = 10;

    void OnTriggerEnter2D(Collider2D other)
    {
        if (other.CompareTag("Player"))
        {
            ScoreManager scoreManager =
            FindObjectOfType<ScoreManager>();
            scoreManager.AddScore(scoreValue);
            Destroy(gameObject);
        }
    }
}
```

Explanation of the Script:

- **OnTriggerEnter2D**: This method detects when another collider enters the trigger's area.
- **CompareTag**: Ensures the collider interacting with the trigger is tagged as "Player."
- **ScoreManager**: Calls a method in ScoreManager to update the score. After updating the score, the object is removed from the Scene.

Tagging the Player:

- Select the Player GameObject in the Hierarchy and set its **Tag** to "Player" in the Inspector to ensure it's recognized by the trigger.

Step 3: Handling Collisions with Colliders

Unlike triggers, standard colliders respond with a physical interaction when they come into contact. For example, if the player character collides with an enemy, it might bounce back or lose health.

Collision Detection Script

Create a script that handles collision interactions. In this example, we'll make the player take damage upon colliding with an enemy.

```csharp
using UnityEngine;

public class Enemy : MonoBehaviour
{
    public int damage = 1;

    void OnCollisionEnter2D(Collision2D collision)
    {
        if (collision.gameObject.CompareTag("Player"))
        {
            PlayerHealth playerHealth =
            collision.gameObject.GetComponent<PlayerHealth>();
            playerHealth.TakeDamage(damage);
        }
    }
}
```

Explanation of the Script:

- **OnCollisionEnter2D**: Detects physical contact with the player.
- **TakeDamage()**: Calls a method on the PlayerHealth script to reduce the player's health.

Adding a PlayerHealth Script

To support the damage system, add a **PlayerHealth** script that manages the player's health and handles taking damage.

```csharp
using UnityEngine;

public class PlayerHealth : MonoBehaviour
{
    public int health = 3;

    public void TakeDamage(int amount)
    {
        health -= amount;
        if (health <= 0)
        {
            Die();
        }
    }

    void Die()
    {
        Debug.Log("Player has died.");
        // Additional death handling logic, like restarting the
        level
    }
}
```

Explanation of the Script:

- **TakeDamage()**: Reduces health based on the damage taken and checks if health is zero.
- **Die()**: Called when health reaches zero, triggering game-over actions like resetting the level or displaying a game-over screen.

Testing the Interaction:

- Enter Play mode and test by moving the player to collide with the enemy. Confirm that health decreases upon collision.

Unity's 2D physics system and collision mechanics are key to creating interactive and realistic gameplay. By using Rigidbody2D and Collider2D components, you can simulate gravity, detect collisions, and implement triggers to create dynamic, engaging experiences. Whether managing player health, creating pickups, or triggering animations, these foundational techniques allow you to add depth to your game and provide responsive feedback to player actions. With these skills, you can expand on your game's interactions, introducing more complex mechanics like platforms, traps, and environmental effects.

Building a Platformer Game: Concepts and Setup

Platformer games are a classic genre where players navigate levels by jumping, climbing, and avoiding obstacles. Designing a platformer involves creating interactive environments, adding characters with responsive controls, and implementing obstacles and collectibles to engage players. In this section, we'll guide you through building a simple platformer game in Unity, covering essential concepts and step-by-step setup.

Level Design and Backgrounds for Platformers

The foundation of any platformer game is its level design. Levels in a platformer are often structured as sequences of platforms, paths, and interactive elements. The backgrounds provide visual depth and context, enhancing the immersive experience.

Step 1: Setting Up the Scene and Background
Create a New Scene:

- Start by creating a new scene in Unity and name it PlatformerLevel1.

- Set the Scene view to **2D** mode for easier visualization.

Add a Background:

- Import a background image or texture suitable for the platformer's theme (e.g., a forest, cave, or cityscape).
- Drag the background image into the Scene from the **Assets** folder. Adjust its position and scale to cover the camera view.

Layering Backgrounds for Depth:

- To add visual depth, consider using multiple layers for your background. For example, you can create layers for foreground elements, middleground elements, and distant backgrounds.
- Set each background layer's **Order in Layer** in the **Sprite Renderer** component to define its position relative to other objects.

Step 2: Designing the Platforms
Create Platforms Using Sprites:

- Import platform sprites or create basic shapes to serve as platforms.
- Drag a platform sprite into the Scene and position it where the player can jump onto it.
- Duplicate and arrange platforms to form pathways, jumps, and obstacles, ensuring they're reachable and varied for an engaging level design.

Add Colliders to Platforms:

- Select each platform and attach a **Box Collider 2D** component from the Inspector. This collider will prevent the player from passing through the platforms and enable collision-based interactions.

Organizing Platforms in the Hierarchy:

- For clarity, create an empty GameObject named Platforms in the Hierarchy and make all platform objects children of it.

Step 3: Using Tilemaps for Level Design

Unity's **Tilemap** feature can simplify level creation by letting you paint platforms and obstacles directly into the Scene. Tilemaps are especially useful for grid-based platformers with repetitive elements like bricks or ground tiles.

Create a Tilemap:

- Go to **GameObject > 2D Object > Tilemap > Rectangular** to create a Tilemap and Grid.
- Import tile images into Unity, convert them to **Sprite (2D and UI)** format, and add them to the Tile Palette (Window > 2D > Tile Palette).

Painting Tiles:

- Use the Tile Palette to select tiles and paint them into the Tilemap in the Scene. Tilemaps allow you to quickly adjust level layouts and add visual detail.

Adding a Controllable Character and Movement Controls

Now that the level layout is established, we'll add a controllable character and implement movement controls. These controls should feel responsive and include basic platforming mechanics like jumping and walking.

Step 1: Creating the Player Character
Add a Player Sprite:

- Import a character sprite or use a basic shape to represent the player.
- Drag the sprite into the Scene and name the GameObject Player.

Attach a Rigidbody2D Component:

- Select the Player GameObject and go to **Add Component > Physics 2D > Rigidbody2D**.
- Set the **Gravity Scale** to around 2 to allow realistic falling speed while maintaining control.

Attach a Collider:

- Add a **Box Collider 2D** or **Circle Collider 2D** to the player. Adjust the collider's size to match the player's sprite for accurate collision detection.

Step 2: Writing the Player Movement Script

Create a script to control the player's movement and jumping. This script will capture keyboard input and translate it into character movement.

Create a PlayerController Script:

- In the **Scripts** folder, create a new script called PlayerController.
- Attach this script to the Player GameObject.

Implement the Movement and Jumping Logic

Here's an example script to add basic movement and jumping:

```csharp
using UnityEngine;

public class PlayerController : MonoBehaviour
{
    private Rigidbody2D rb;
    public float moveSpeed = 5f;
    public float jumpForce = 10f;
    private bool isGrounded;

    void Start()
    {
```

```csharp
        rb = GetComponent<Rigidbody2D>();
    }

    void Update()
    {
        // Movement
        float horizontalInput = Input.GetAxis("Horizontal");
        rb.velocity = new Vector2(horizontalInput * moveSpeed,
        rb.velocity.y);

        // Jumping
        if (Input.GetKeyDown(KeyCode.Space) && isGrounded)
        {
            rb.AddForce(Vector2.up * jumpForce,
            ForceMode2D.Impulse);
            isGrounded = false;
        }
    }

    private void OnCollisionEnter2D(Collision2D collision)
    {
        // Check if player lands on ground
        if (collision.gameObject.CompareTag("Platform"))
        {
            isGrounded = true;
        }
    }
}
```

Explanation of the Script:

- **moveSpeed**: Controls horizontal movement speed.
- **jumpForce**: Determines the upward force applied for jumps.
- **isGrounded**: Boolean that tracks whether the player is on the ground. This prevents double-jumping.
- **OnCollisionEnter2D**: Detects when the player lands on a platform, allowing them to jump again.

Testing the Controls:

- Press **Play** to test movement and jumping. Adjust **moveSpeed** and **jumpForce** in the Inspector to fine-tune the feel of the controls.

Implementing Basic Obstacles and Collectibles

Obstacles and collectibles add gameplay elements that increase challenge and reward the player.

Step 1: Adding Collectibles
Create a Collectible Sprite:

- Import a sprite to represent a collectible item, such as a coin or star.
- Drag it into the Scene and add a **Circle Collider 2D** component. Enable **Is Trigger** so the player can pass through it.

Write a Collectible Script

Create a script to add points to the player's score upon collection.

```csharp
using UnityEngine;

public class Collectible : MonoBehaviour
{
    public int scoreValue = 10;

    void OnTriggerEnter2D(Collider2D other)
    {
        if (other.CompareTag("Player"))
        {
            ScoreManager scoreManager =
            FindObjectOfType<ScoreManager>();
            scoreManager.AddScore(scoreValue);
            Destroy(gameObject);
```

```
        }
     }
}
```

Explanation of the Script:

- **OnTriggerEnter2D**: Detects when the player collides with the collectible.
- **ScoreManager**: Updates the score when a collectible is picked up, then destroys the collectible.

Step 2: Adding Obstacles
Create Obstacle Objects:

- Import or create obstacle sprites (e.g., spikes or pits) and add them to the Scene.
- Attach a **Box Collider 2D** to each obstacle for collision detection.

Implement Damage on Collision
Create a script to reduce the player's health upon colliding with obstacles.

```csharp
using UnityEngine;

public class Obstacle : MonoBehaviour
{
    public int damage = 1;

    void OnCollisionEnter2D(Collision2D collision)
    {
        if (collision.gameObject.CompareTag("Player"))
        {
            PlayerHealth playerHealth =
            collision.gameObject.GetComponent<PlayerHealth>();
```

DIVING DEEPER INTO UNITY'S 2D CAPABILITIES

```
            playerHealth.TakeDamage(damage);
        }
    }
}
```

Explanation of the Script:

- **TakeDamage**: Reduces player health when they collide with an obstacle, allowing you to create hazards that add challenge to the level.

Tagging the Player:

- Ensure the Player is tagged as "Player" in the Inspector to allow the scripts to recognize it.

Step 3: Testing Collectibles and Obstacles

Play the Scene: Test the level by moving through it and interacting with collectibles and obstacles.

Debugging: If collisions or pickups don't work as expected, verify collider setups and script logic.

By following these steps, you've set up a basic platformer level with interactive elements, including controllable character movement, platforms, obstacles, and collectibles. These fundamentals provide a strong base to expand upon, allowing you to add additional mechanics, refine controls, and introduce new challenges. With these foundational skills, you're equipped to create engaging platformer experiences that test players' timing, precision, and problem-solving abilities.

Hands-On Project: Simple 2D Platformer with Scoring

This hands-on project will guide you through building a simple 2D platformer game in Unity that includes movement, obstacles, collectibles, and a scoring system. This project will reinforce your understanding of 2D physics, scripting, and UI setup.

Project Overview

In this platformer, the player will navigate a level by jumping across platforms, avoiding obstacles, and collecting items to gain points. The score will update in real-time, providing feedback on the player's progress.

Step 1: Setting Up the Scene
  Create a New Scene:

- Open Unity, go to **File > New Scene**, and name it Simple2DPlatformer.

Switch to 2D Mode:

- Set the Scene view to **2D** to make it easier to place and arrange 2D objects.

Add a Background:

- Import a background image and drag it into the Scene. Adjust its position and scale as needed.

Create Platforms:

- Import or create a platform sprite. Drag it into the Scene to create a GameObject, and name it Platform.
- Duplicate the platform by pressing **Ctrl + D** or **Cmd + D** and arrange them to create a path through the level.
- Attach **Box Collider 2D** components to each platform so the player can land on them.

Step 2: Adding a Player Character

Create a Player Sprite:

- Import a player sprite or use a simple shape. Drag it into the Scene and rename it Player.

Add Rigidbody2D and Collider:

- Attach a **Rigidbody2D** component to make the player character subject to gravity.
- Set **Gravity Scale** to around 2 to allow realistic falling while maintaining control.
- Add a **Box Collider 2D** to detect collisions with platforms and other objects.

Create a PlayerController Script

Create a script to control the player's movement and jumping.

```csharp
using UnityEngine;

public class PlayerController : MonoBehaviour
{
    private Rigidbody2D rb;
    public float moveSpeed = 5f;
    public float jumpForce = 10f;
    private bool isGrounded;

    void Start()
    {
        rb = GetComponent<Rigidbody2D>();
    }

    void Update()
    {
        // Horizontal movement
```

```csharp
        float horizontalInput = Input.GetAxis("Horizontal");
        rb.velocity = new Vector2(horizontalInput * moveSpeed,
        rb.velocity.y);

        // Jumping
        if (Input.GetKeyDown(KeyCode.Space) && isGrounded)
        {
            rb.AddForce(Vector2.up * jumpForce,
            ForceMode2D.Impulse);
            isGrounded = false;
        }
    }

    private void OnCollisionEnter2D(Collision2D collision)
    {
        if (collision.gameObject.CompareTag("Platform"))
        {
            isGrounded = true;
        }
    }
}
```

Attach the Script:

- Attach PlayerController to the Player GameObject and adjust **moveSpeed** and **jumpForce** in the Inspector as needed.

Step 3: Adding Obstacles and Collectibles
Adding Obstacles
Create an Obstacle Sprite:

- Import an obstacle sprite, such as spikes. Drag it into the Scene to create an obstacle GameObject, and rename it Obstacle.
- Add a **Box Collider 2D** or **Polygon Collider 2D** to the obstacle and adjust it to fit the sprite.

Create an Obstacle Script

Add a script to deal damage or reset the player position on collision.

```csharp
using UnityEngine;

public class Obstacle : MonoBehaviour
{
    private void OnCollisionEnter2D(Collision2D collision)
    {
        if (collision.gameObject.CompareTag("Player"))
        {
            PlayerHealth playerHealth =
            collision.gameObject.GetComponent<PlayerHealth>();
            playerHealth.TakeDamage(1);
        }
    }
}
```

Tagging and Testing:

- Tag the Player GameObject as Player to allow the obstacle script to detect it correctly.

Adding Collectibles
Create a Collectible Sprite:

- Import a collectible sprite, such as a coin. Drag it into the Scene and name it Collectible.
- Add a **Circle Collider 2D** to the collectible and enable **Is Trigger** to make it a trigger collider.

Create a Collectible Script
Write a script to add points to the player's score when they collect it.

```csharp
csharp

using UnityEngine;

public class Collectible : MonoBehaviour
{
    public int scoreValue = 10;

    void OnTriggerEnter2D(Collider2D other)
    {
        if (other.CompareTag("Player"))
        {
            ScoreManager scoreManager =
            FindObjectOfType<ScoreManager>();
            scoreManager.AddScore(scoreValue);
            Destroy(gameObject);
        }
    }
}
```

Attach and Test the Script:

- Attach the script to each collectible GameObject and test the Scene to ensure collectibles disappear upon collection.

Step 4: Setting Up the Scoring System
Create a UI Text Element for Score:

- In the Hierarchy, go to **GameObject > UI > Text** to create a UI text element.
- Rename it ScoreText and adjust its position and font settings.

Create a ScoreManager Script
Add a script to manage and display the player's score.

```csharp

using UnityEngine;
using UnityEngine.UI;

public class ScoreManager : MonoBehaviour
{
    public Text scoreText;
    private int score = 0;

    public void AddScore(int value)
    {
        score += value;
        scoreText.text = "Score: " + score;
    }
}
```

Link ScoreText to ScoreManager:

- Create an empty GameObject named GameManager in the Hierarchy and attach the ScoreManager script.
- Drag ScoreText from the Hierarchy into the scoreText field in the ScoreManager component in the Inspector.

Step 5: Testing and Balancing the Game
Testing Movement and Interaction:

- Enter Play mode and navigate through the level, checking that the player can jump, collide with obstacles, and collect items.

Adjust Parameters:

- Fine-tune **moveSpeed** and **jumpForce** for smooth controls.
- Adjust **scoreValue** in the Collectible script to control how many points each collectible is worth.
- Test obstacle interactions to ensure they are challenging but fair.

Debugging:

- If any interaction doesn't work as expected, review colliders, tags, and references in the Inspector to verify correct settings.

By completing this project, you've built a simple but functional 2D platformer with a scoring system, providing a foundation for more complex mechanics and features. You've used key concepts like Rigidbody2D, Collider2D, triggers, and UI to bring interactivity and feedback to the game. This platformer serves as a template for adding further complexity, such as advanced movement, power-ups, enemies, or multi-level progression.

Introduction to Unity's 3D Environment

U nity's 3D environment provides tools and features for creating complex, interactive 3D experiences. Setting up a 3D scene, configuring a project, and managing 3D GameObjects are essential skills for building immersive worlds. This chapter covers how to set up a new 3D scene, configure project settings, and manipulate 3D GameObjects to lay the foundation for any 3D project in Unity.

Setting Up a 3D Scene

In Unity, a 3D scene is a virtual space where objects, lighting, and other elements come together to create a game level or environment. The setup process involves arranging objects, configuring lighting, and setting up the camera to define how players will experience the game world.

1. Creating a New 3D Scene
   Open Unity Hub:

- Launch Unity Hub and select **New Project** to start from scratch.

Select the 3D Template:

- Choose the **3D Core** template for general-purpose 3D games, **Universal Render Pipeline (URP)** for optimized graphics across platforms, or **High Definition Render Pipeline (HDRP)** for high-quality visuals suited to advanced hardware.

- Enter a project name, specify the location, and click **Create Project** to initialize.

Save the Scene:

- Once Unity loads the project, go to **File > Save As** to save your first scene. Name it descriptively, like MainLevel or GameWorld.

2. Navigating the Scene View

Unity's **Scene view** is the workspace where you position, manipulate, and organize 3D objects. Navigation in the Scene view is key to efficiently designing your environment:

- **Move Tool (W)**: Enables you to drag objects along the X, Y, and Z axes.
- **Rotate Tool (E)**: Rotates objects around each axis, useful for adjusting orientation.
- **Scale Tool (R)**: Scales objects along individual axes or uniformly.
- **Transform Gizmo**: Located at the top of the Scene view, it provides visual controls for position, rotation, and scale.

Unity's coordinate system follows a **left-handed system** where:

- **X-axis** is horizontal.
- **Y-axis** is vertical.
- **Z-axis** represents depth (forward-backward in the Scene view).

Understanding this coordinate system is critical for placing objects accurately and defining movement or interactions in your 3D game.

Creating and Configuring a 3D Project

Configuring your 3D project settings ensures that your environment performs well and looks polished. Unity offers numerous options for configuring rendering, lighting, and physics, each of which can greatly impact the look and feel of a 3D project.

1. Basic Project Settings
Rendering Pipeline:

- For the 3D Core template, Unity uses the **Built-in Rendering Pipeline** by default, suitable for simpler 3D games. URP and HDRP can be enabled later for higher performance or visual fidelity.
- If you chose URP or HDRP during setup, Unity has already configured the appropriate settings.

Setting Up Layers and Tags:

- **Tags** are used to categorize objects for identification, such as "Player" or "Enemy."
- **Layers** are useful for grouping objects by collision rules or visibility. For example, you might create layers for "Environment" or "Interactive" to differentiate collision behaviors.

Physics Settings:

- Go to **Edit > Project Settings > Physics** to access physics settings like gravity and collision layers.
- Gravity is typically set to -9.81 on the Y-axis for realistic falling speeds. Adjust collision layers to control which objects interact with each other in your scene.

2. Configuring Lighting for Realistic Effects
Lighting is crucial in creating a believable 3D environment. Unity offers several types of lights, each suited to different purposes, such as general scene illumination, highlights, or special effects.
Types of Lights:

- **Directional Light**: Used for global lighting, simulating sunlight. This type of light affects the entire scene and is ideal for outdoor settings.
- **Point Light**: Emits light in all directions from a single point. Commonly used for localized lighting like lanterns or torches.
- **Spot Light**: Casts light in a cone shape, useful for directional light sources such as flashlights or headlights.
- **Area Light** (HDRP only): Spreads light evenly from a rectangular source, commonly used indoors.

Adjusting Light Settings:

- Select a light in the **Hierarchy** and adjust its **Intensity, Color,** and **Range** in the Inspector.
- For natural shadows, enable **Shadows** and choose between **Hard Shadows** or **Soft Shadows** depending on the look you want.

Lighting Settings Panel:

- Go to **Window > Rendering > Lighting** to open the Lighting Settings panel, where you can configure ambient lighting, baked lighting for static lights, and enable **Fog** for atmospheric depth.

3. Configuring the Main Camera

The **Main Camera** determines the player's viewpoint in the game. Configuring the camera position, rotation, and field of view (FOV) is critical for establishing how players will perceive and interact with the game environment.

Position and Rotate the Camera:

- Move the camera in the Scene view to frame the main area where players will start or where primary gameplay happens. Positioning the camera slightly above and angled downward works well for many game types.

Camera Settings:

- **Field of View (FOV)**: Determines the breadth of the scene visible to the player. A typical FOV for 3D games is 60-90 degrees.
- **Clipping Planes**: The **Near** and **Far** clipping planes set the minimum and maximum render distances, helping to optimize rendering by excluding far-away objects.

Adding Multiple Cameras:

- You can add additional cameras for different perspectives or functions, like a minimap or cinematic sequences. Configure each camera separately and toggle them based on gameplay needs.

Adding and Manipulating 3D GameObjects

3D GameObjects are the building blocks of any scene, from simple geometric shapes to complex models with materials and animations. Learning to create, place, and manipulate these objects is foundational to creating interactive 3D environments.

1. Creating Primitive 3D GameObjects

Unity provides several primitive shapes for building scenes, such as **Cubes**, **Spheres**, **Capsules**, and **Planes**. These are useful for prototyping and setting up the basic layout of the scene.

Adding a Primitive:

- Go to **GameObject > 3D Object** and select a shape (e.g., Cube, Sphere, Plane).
- Name the GameObject descriptively in the **Hierarchy** to keep the scene organized.

Transforming GameObjects:

- **Position**: Use the **Move Tool** (W) to adjust the object's position along the X, Y, and Z axes.
- **Rotation**: Use the **Rotate Tool** (E) to orient the object in the Scene. Rotation is particularly important for elements like cameras or characters.
- **Scale**: Use the **Scale Tool** (R) to adjust the object's size. Scaling can be uniform (all axes) or individual, depending on your needs.

2. Importing and Using 3D Models

In addition to primitives, you can import custom 3D models created in external software like Blender or Maya.

Import the Model:

- Drag your model file (e.g., .fbx or .obj) from your file system into Unity's **Assets** folder.
- Unity will recognize the model, and it can be added to the Scene by dragging it from the Assets folder.

Applying Materials and Textures:

- Create or import **Materials** and drag them onto the model to change its appearance.
- Adjust properties like **Color**, **Metallic**, and **Smoothness** in the Inspector for visual detail.

3. Working with Rigidbodies and Colliders

Rigidbodies and Colliders bring physics-based interaction to your 3D objects, allowing them to move, collide, and respond to forces.

Adding a Rigidbody Component:

- Select a GameObject, go to **Add Component > Physics > Rigidbody**.
- Configure properties like **Mass** and **Drag** to control how the object behaves in a physics-based environment.

Adding Colliders:

- Unity provides various Collider types, including **Box Collider**, **Sphere Collider**, and **Mesh Collider** for custom shapes.
- Attach a collider to define the shape of the collision boundary, enabling interaction with other objects.

Setting Up Triggers:

- Enable **Is Trigger** on a Collider to make it a trigger, allowing objects to pass through while still detecting collisions. This is useful for areas like checkpoints, item pickups, or other interactive zones.

4. Prefabs for Reusability

Prefabs are reusable GameObjects that retain their properties, allowing you to duplicate them consistently throughout your project.

Creating a Prefab:

- Drag a GameObject from the Hierarchy into the **Project** window to create a prefab. Prefabs can be customized and saved for later use.

Editing Prefabs:

- Open **Prefab Mode** by double-clicking a prefab in the Project window. Any changes made in Prefab Mode will apply to all instances of that prefab across your scenes.

By setting up a 3D scene, configuring project settings, and adding and manipulating GameObjects, you're establishing a foundation for building immersive and interactive 3D environments in Unity. Understanding these essentials will allow you to populate your world with objects, manage lighting and physics, and create complex scenes that bring your game to life.

Lighting, Shadows, and Materials in 3D

In Unity, effective use of lighting, shadows, and materials enhances the realism and atmosphere of a 3D environment. The lighting system in Unity includes various light types and shadow options, each contributing to the overall look and feel of your scene. Materials and shaders define how surfaces respond to light, impacting texture, reflectivity, and color. This section will cover the basics of Unity's lighting system, shadow management, and material and shader setup to help you create visually compelling 3D scenes.

Understanding Unity's Lighting System

Unity's lighting system includes several light types that simulate real-world lighting conditions. Each light type is designed for specific use cases, such as global illumination, focused spotlights, and localized point lights.

Types of Lights in Unity
Directional Light:

- Simulates sunlight and affects all objects in the scene as if they're evenly lit from one direction. Ideal for outdoor scenes.
- Adjust the rotation to control the light's angle and simulate different times of day.

Point Light:

- Emits light in all directions from a single point, similar to a light bulb. It's suitable for indoor lighting or small, localized light sources.
- Adjust **Range** to control how far the light reaches and **Intensity** to set the brightness.

Spot Light:

- Projects a cone-shaped beam, useful for creating focused light sources, like flashlights or stage lights.

- Use **Spot Angle** to define the width of the light cone and **Range** to set its reach.

Area Light (HDRP only):

- Emits light from a rectangular surface, offering a soft, even illumination for larger areas. Often used for simulating windows or overhead lights.

Configuring Light Settings

Each light has customizable settings that control how it affects objects in the scene:

- **Intensity**: Sets the brightness of the light. Higher values increase brightness, while lower values dim the light.
- **Color**: Determines the light's color, which affects the mood of the scene. For example, warm colors (yellow/orange) suggest a cozy setting, while cool colors (blue/white) create a sterile or eerie effect.
- **Range** (Point and Spot Lights): Defines the distance the light travels before fading out. A shorter range is better for tight spaces, while longer ranges illuminate larger areas.
- **Spot Angle** (Spot Light only): Controls the angle of the light cone, affecting the spread of light.

Understanding Shadows

Shadows add depth and realism to 3D scenes by simulating the way objects block light. Unity offers shadow options that vary in realism and performance impact.

Shadow Types:

- **Hard Shadows**: Produce sharp edges and are less computationally demanding. Use for a stylized or low-resource look.
- **Soft Shadows**: Create softer edges that blend more naturally, requiring more processing power but looking more realistic.

Shadow Settings in Lights:

- **Shadow Type**: Select **None** for no shadows, **Hard Shadows** for defined edges, or **Soft Shadows** for a more natural look.
- **Strength**: Controls shadow darkness. Setting a low value makes shadows appear lighter, while higher values make them darker and more distinct.
- **Bias** and **Normal Bias**: These settings prevent shadow artifacts, such as shadow acne, by adjusting how close an object must be to cast or receive a shadow.

Real-Time vs. Baked Shadows:

- **Real-Time Shadows**: Generated at runtime and used for dynamic objects, such as characters or objects that move.
- **Baked Shadows**: Precomputed during the development process and do not change at runtime. Ideal for static objects, as baked shadows reduce processing requirements and improve performance.

Global Lighting Settings

Unity's global lighting settings allow you to configure ambient light, reflections, and other environmental lighting options:

Ambient Lighting:

- Controls the base lighting level in the scene. You can access this in **Window > Rendering > Lighting > Environment**. Ambient lighting helps fill in shadows and prevents overly dark areas.
- **Color** and **Intensity** settings allow you to adjust the overall brightness and color of ambient light.

Environment Reflections:

- Environment reflections add realism by simulating light bouncing off objects. Adjust **Reflection Intensity** and **Bounces** for complex reflections.

Fog:

- Adds atmospheric depth by blending distant objects with the background color. Enable **Fog** in **Lighting Settings** and set **Density** and **Color** to create effects like mist or haze.

Lighting Modes:

- Unity provides options for **Mixed Lighting**, which combines real-time and baked lighting. This setup is efficient, allowing static objects to use baked lighting while dynamic objects receive real-time lighting.

Basic Materials and Shaders

Materials and shaders determine the appearance of surfaces, from their color to their reflectivity and texture. Materials use shaders to control how they interact with light, enabling a wide range of visual effects.

Creating and Applying Materials

A **Material** is an asset that defines the surface appearance of an object. Materials assign color, texture, and other visual properties to GameObjects.

Creating a Material:

- In the **Project** window, right-click and select **Create > Material**. Give the material a descriptive name (e.g., MetalMaterial or BrickTexture).
- Open the material in the **Inspector** to access its properties, where you can adjust color, texture, and other settings.

Applying a Material to a GameObject:

- Drag the material from the Project window onto a GameObject in the

Scene or Hierarchy to apply it.

- The material's properties are immediately visible on the object, allowing you to preview its appearance in real-time.

Material Properties
Albedo:

- Defines the base color or texture of the material. Use the color picker or assign a texture map for more detailed surfaces, such as wood or stone.

Metallic and Smoothness:

- **Metallic**: Sets how metallic or reflective the material appears. Higher values make the material look more like metal, reflecting more light.
- **Smoothness**: Controls the glossiness of the surface. Lower values create a rough, matte finish, while higher values give a shiny, polished look.

Normal Maps:

- Normal maps add surface detail by simulating small bumps and grooves without altering the object's geometry. This effect creates the illusion of texture depth and is commonly used for materials like bricks or rough metal.

Emission:

- Emission allows a material to emit its own light, making it appear self-illuminated. This effect is useful for screens, neon lights, or glowing objects.

Understanding Shaders
A **Shader** is a program that determines how a material reacts to light

and how it is rendered. Unity includes several shader types, each offering different visual effects:

Standard Shader:

- Unity's default shader, providing a range of controls for realistic materials. The Standard Shader works well for most surfaces, from metals to fabrics.

Unlit Shader:

- This shader does not interact with lighting, making it suitable for UI elements, backgrounds, or objects that should remain unaffected by scene lighting.

Transparent Shader:

- Allows materials to render with partial or full transparency, useful for glass, water, or translucent materials.

Custom Shaders:

- Custom shaders allow for unique effects, such as animated textures or environmental effects. Unity's Shader Graph (URP and HDRP) provides a node-based tool for creating custom shaders visually without coding.

Using Shader Graph for Custom Materials (URP and HDRP)

Unity's **Shader Graph** is a visual tool for creating complex shaders without code, available for URP and HDRP projects. Shader Graph lets you connect nodes that control different aspects of the material, such as color, reflectivity, and opacity.

Creating a Shader Graph:

- In the Project window, right-click and choose **Create > Shader > PBR**

Graph (for physically-based rendering). Name the shader graph and open it in the Shader Graph editor.

Adding Nodes:

- Shader Graph uses nodes that connect to control properties like color, texture, and reflectivity. For example, connect an **Albedo** node to set the material's base color or add a **Normal Map** node for texture depth.

Preview and Apply:

- Preview the material in the Shader Graph window and adjust nodes to refine the appearance. Save and apply the shader to a material, which you can then use on GameObjects in your scene.

Mastering Unity's lighting, shadow, and material systems is essential for creating visually rich and immersive 3D environments. With an understanding of lighting types, shadow options, and material properties, you can shape the look and feel of your scenes to match any style or atmosphere. Experimenting with shaders and materials lets you customize surfaces to achieve specific visual effects, adding depth and realism to your projects. These tools form the basis for creating environments that feel lifelike, guiding players' focus and enhancing the storytelling within your 3D worlds.

Camera Setup and Controls

In a 3D environment, the camera determines the player's view of the world, influencing both gameplay and the overall experience. Correctly positioning and controlling the camera enhances immersion and ensures players see the necessary elements for interaction. Unity's flexible camera settings and scripting capabilities allow you to create dynamic camera movements, adjust perspective, and follow objects like the player character.

Positioning and Adjusting the Camera for 3D Views

Unity's **Main Camera** offers several settings to define how the player sees the game world. Positioning and configuring the camera involves understanding Unity's coordinate system, adjusting camera properties, and experimenting with different perspectives to create the desired visual effect.

1. Understanding Camera Placement and Orientation

In Unity's 3D space, the camera's position and rotation directly affect the player's perspective:

- **Position**: Defines the camera's location in the scene along the X, Y, and Z axes. The camera should be placed at a suitable distance from the main subject (e.g., the player) to frame the gameplay area.
- **Rotation**: Controls the camera's orientation, determining the angle from which it views objects. Rotating the camera allows you to capture different perspectives, such as over-the-shoulder or top-down views.

To adjust the camera in the Scene view:

- Select the **Main Camera** in the **Hierarchy**.
- Use the **Move Tool** (W) to adjust its position along the X, Y, and Z axes.
- Use the **Rotate Tool** (E) to orient the camera toward the subject. The Z-axis usually points in the forward direction, so rotating the camera along the X-axis is common for angled views.

2. Configuring Camera Properties

Unity's Main Camera has several properties in the **Inspector** that allow you to customize the field of view, depth, and rendering options.

Field of View (FOV):

- The FOV setting adjusts the camera's viewing angle, affecting how much of the scene is visible. A wider FOV (e.g., 90 degrees) shows more of the scene, creating a sense of space, while a narrower FOV (e.g., 60 degrees) brings objects closer, which is common for first-person perspectives.

Clipping Planes:

- The **Near** and **Far Clipping Planes** define the minimum and maximum render distances. Objects closer than the Near plane or farther than the Far plane are not rendered, helping optimize performance.
- For example, setting Near to 0.1 and Far to 1000 ensures the camera displays objects at close distances while still showing distant backgrounds.

Projection Mode:

- **Perspective**: Creates realistic 3D depth, where objects appear smaller as they move farther from the camera. Perspective projection is used for most 3D games.
- **Orthographic**: Removes depth and renders objects at the same size regardless of distance. Orthographic mode is commonly used for 2D and certain stylized 3D games, such as isometric views.

Background Color:

- Sets the color shown in the background when no objects are rendered. Adjust the color to match the environment or add a skybox for a more realistic backdrop.

Skybox:

- Unity allows you to assign a **Skybox** material to the camera, creating a background that simulates the sky, clouds, or space. This effect is ideal for outdoor scenes and enhances realism.

Basic Camera Scripts for Following Player Movement

Creating a camera that follows the player's movements enhances immersion and maintains focus on the action. Unity's scripting system allows you to control the camera's position, smoothly track player movement, and customize the follow behavior to suit the game style.

Step 1: Setting Up the Camera Follow Script

A basic camera-follow script will keep the camera at a fixed distance from the player while dynamically updating its position as the player moves.

Create a New Script:

- In the **Scripts** folder, right-click and select **Create > C# Script**. Name it CameraFollow.
- Attach this script to the **Main Camera** in the Hierarchy.

Writing the CameraFollow Script

This script will maintain a constant offset between the camera and the player, updating the camera's position as the player moves.

```csharp
using UnityEngine;

public class CameraFollow : MonoBehaviour
{
    public Transform player; // Reference to the player's
    transform
    public Vector3 offset;    // Offset distance between the
    player and camera
    public float smoothSpeed = 0.125f; // Smooth transition speed

    void LateUpdate()
    {
        // Calculate target position
        Vector3 targetPosition = player.position + offset;
```

```
    // Smoothly transition to target position
    Vector3 smoothedPosition =
    Vector3.Lerp(transform.position, targetPosition,
    smoothSpeed);

    // Apply position to camera
    transform.position = smoothedPosition;
  }
}
```

Explanation of the Script:

- **player**: A public variable to assign the player's Transform component in the Inspector.
- **offset**: Determines the fixed distance between the camera and the player.
- **smoothSpeed**: Controls the speed of the camera's movement, allowing for smooth following rather than sudden jumps.
- **LateUpdate()**: Ensures the camera updates after the player has moved, reducing jittery movement.

Setting up the Script in the Inspector:

- In the Inspector for the Main Camera, drag the player GameObject into the **Player** field of the script.
- Adjust the **Offset** value based on the desired camera position relative to the player.
- Tweak **Smooth Speed** to control the camera's responsiveness to player movement.

Step 2: Enhancing the Follow Script with Rotation (Optional)

In some 3D games, the camera may need to rotate to maintain a specific angle relative to the player's orientation. Adding rotation tracking ensures the camera's rotation adjusts as the player turns.

Modifying the CameraFollow Script for Rotation

Add code to track the player's rotation along with position, creating a camera that orbits the player.

```csharp
using UnityEngine;

public class CameraFollow : MonoBehaviour
{
    public Transform player;
    public Vector3 offset;
    public float smoothSpeed = 0.125f;
    public bool followRotation = true; // Option to follow
    player's rotation

    void LateUpdate()
    {
        Vector3 targetPosition = player.position + offset;
        Vector3 smoothedPosition =
        Vector3.Lerp(transform.position, targetPosition,
        smoothSpeed);
        transform.position = smoothedPosition;

        if (followRotation)
        {
            transform.LookAt(player); // Keeps the camera facing
            the player
        }
    }
}
```

Explanation of the Updated Script:

- **followRotation**: A toggle to determine if the camera should track the player's rotation.
- **LookAt**: Points the camera at the player's position, ensuring it's always

149

oriented toward the player.

Step 3: Testing and Adjusting Camera Behavior
Adjusting Offset and Smooth Speed:

- Test different **Offset** values to get the right view angle, distance, and height.
- Increase or decrease **Smooth Speed** to find a balance between responsiveness and smoothness.

Exploring Additional Camera Effects:

- Experiment with adding constraints, such as limiting camera rotation or zooming based on distance to the player, to fit the needs of your game.

Configuring and scripting cameras is essential to guiding player focus and enhancing the gameplay experience in Unity's 3D environment. By adjusting the camera's position, FOV, and clipping planes, you can establish an optimal view of the game world. Creating a follow camera through basic scripting adds an extra layer of polish, ensuring the camera keeps up with the player's movements and maintains an ideal perspective for interaction. Experimenting with advanced camera behaviors can elevate gameplay, giving players a seamless, immersive view of your 3D world.

Building a Simple 3D Maze Game

Creating a 3D maze game in Unity provides an excellent way to explore basic game design elements, such as designing levels, managing player controls, setting up camera mechanics, and implementing game objectives like timers. This section will guide you through building a simple 3D maze game with these core features.

Designing the Maze and Setting Up Collisions

The maze environment is the central structure of the game. It consists of walls, pathways, and possibly traps or checkpoints. Building a maze requires arranging these elements and ensuring that players can interact with them accurately through collision detection.

Step 1: Creating the Maze Structure
Using Basic Primitives for Walls:

- Unity's **Cube** primitive is ideal for building maze walls. To start, create a 3D Cube (GameObject > 3D Object > Cube) and scale it along the X, Y, and Z axes to form a wall.
- Adjust the size to achieve the desired thickness and height for maze walls. For instance, set the wall's Y-axis to 3 for height and its X or Z-axis to create the wall's length.

Arranging Walls to Form a Maze Layout:

- Duplicate the wall GameObject (Ctrl + D) and place the copies to form pathways and dead-ends. Use the **Move Tool** to align and position walls in a grid-like pattern or design a custom layout for more complex paths.
- Ensure the walls are positioned accurately by using the Scene view's **Orthographic mode** (toggle with the O key) to create an overhead view, which simplifies alignment.

Grouping Maze Elements:

- Create an empty GameObject named Maze in the Hierarchy. Parent all wall objects to this GameObject to keep the scene organized and allow easy manipulation of the entire maze structure.

Step 2: Setting Up Collisions

Colliders are essential for detecting when the player hits walls or reaches

151

the maze's endpoints.

Adding Colliders to Maze Walls:

- Each wall (Cube) has a **Box Collider** component by default. Ensure it accurately represents the wall's dimensions by checking the collider's bounds in the Inspector.
- Adjust the **Center** or **Size** of the collider if necessary to fit the wall precisely.

Creating an Exit Point:

- Add a GameObject, like a **Plane** or a unique Cube, to mark the maze's end. This exit point can serve as the objective.
- Add a **Collider** component and enable **Is Trigger** on the exit point to detect when the player reaches it without blocking their movement.

Adding Player Controls and Camera Follow Mechanics

Player controls are essential for navigating the maze, while a dynamic camera makes the gameplay experience smoother and more engaging.

Step 1: Creating the Player Character

Using a Simple Primitive as the Player:

- Create a Sphere (GameObject > 3D Object > Sphere) to represent the player. Position it at the maze's starting point and name it Player in the Hierarchy.

Adding Rigidbody and Collider:

- Attach a **Rigidbody** component to the player to enable physics-based movement. Set **Use Gravity** to allow natural fall behavior and **Constraints** to freeze rotation along the X and Z axes, preventing the player from tipping over.

Step 2: Writing the Player Movement Script

Create a script to control player movement using keyboard input.

Create a New Script:

- Right-click in the **Scripts** folder and select **Create > C# Script**. Name it PlayerController and attach it to the Player GameObject.

Writing the Movement Code

Implement basic movement in the script to allow forward, backward, and lateral movement.

```csharp
using UnityEngine;

public class PlayerController : MonoBehaviour
{
    public float speed = 5f;
    private Rigidbody rb;

    void Start()
    {
        rb = GetComponent<Rigidbody>();
    }

    void FixedUpdate()
    {
        // Capture player input
        float moveHorizontal = Input.GetAxis("Horizontal");
        float moveVertical = Input.GetAxis("Vertical");

        // Calculate movement direction and apply speed
        Vector3 movement = new Vector3(moveHorizontal, 0.0f,
        moveVertical) * speed;
        rb.AddForce(movement);
    }
}
```

Explanation of the Script:

- **Input.GetAxis:** Captures player input for horizontal (left/right) and vertical (forward/backward) directions.
- **AddForce:** Applies force to the Rigidbody in the direction of the movement vector, moving the player through the maze.

Adjusting Speed:

- Set the **Speed** value in the Inspector to control the player's movement responsiveness. Experiment with different values to find a suitable pace for navigating the maze.

Step 3: Setting Up the Camera to Follow the Player

A follow camera keeps the player in view, enhancing navigation in the 3D maze.

Creating a Camera Follow Script:

- Create a new script named CameraFollow and attach it to the Main Camera.

Implementing the Follow Logic

The following code will keep the camera at a fixed distance from the player, updating its position as the player moves.

```csharp
using UnityEngine;

public class CameraFollow : MonoBehaviour
{
    public Transform player;
    public Vector3 offset;
```

```
void LateUpdate()
{
    // Update camera position based on player's position with
    an offset
    transform.position = player.position + offset;
}
}
```

Explanation of the Script:

- **LateUpdate()**: Runs after all Update methods, ensuring the camera follows smoothly without jitter.
- **Offset**: Keeps the camera at a set distance from the player, preserving the player's position within the frame.

Adjusting the Offset:

- Experiment with the offset values in the Inspector to achieve the desired camera height and distance. An offset of (0, 10, -10) often works well for an overhead or third-person perspective.

Adding a Timer and Simple Objectives

A timer and objectives enhance the gameplay by challenging players to complete the maze within a set time or collect items before reaching the exit.

Step 1: Implementing a Timer
Creating the Timer UI:

- Go to **GameObject > UI > Text** to create a text element for displaying the timer.
- Rename it TimerText and position it in the upper-left corner of the screen. Adjust the font size and color for readability.

Writing the Timer Script

Create a script named GameTimer and attach it to an empty GameObject called GameManager.

```csharp
using UnityEngine;
using UnityEngine.UI;

public class GameTimer : MonoBehaviour
{
    public Text timerText;
    private float timeRemaining = 60f; // Starting time in seconds
    private bool timerRunning = true;

    void Update()
    {
        if (timerRunning)
        {
            if (timeRemaining > 0)
            {
                timeRemaining -= Time.deltaTime;
                timerText.text = "Time: " +
                Mathf.Ceil(timeRemaining).ToString();
            }
            else
            {
                timerRunning = false;
                timerText.text = "Time's Up!";
                // Additional game-over logic can be implemented
                here
            }
        }
    }
}
```

Explanation of the Script:

- **timeRemaining**: Keeps track of the countdown time.
- **Update()**: Decreases timeRemaining each frame and updates the timer

text. Once time runs out, the timer stops and displays "Time's Up!".

Step 2: Adding Collectibles as Objectives
Creating Collectible Items:

- Use simple objects like **Spheres** or **Cubes** to represent collectibles. Name them descriptively (e.g., Collectible1, Collectible2) and place them in the maze.

Adding a Collectible Script

Write a script that increments a score counter when the player collects an item.

```csharp
using UnityEngine;

public class Collectible : MonoBehaviour
{
    public int scoreValue = 10;

    void OnTriggerEnter(Collider other)
    {
        if (other.CompareTag("Player"))
        {
            ScoreManager scoreManager =
            FindObjectOfType<ScoreManager>();
            scoreManager.AddScore(scoreValue);
            Destroy(gameObject);
        }
    }
}
```

Explanation of the Script:

- **OnTriggerEnter**: Detects when the player collides with the collectible.
- **AddScore**: Calls a method in a **ScoreManager** script to update the

157

score.

Displaying the Score:

- Create a UI text element named ScoreText to display the score. Update it using the **ScoreManager** script.

Step 3: Testing the Game
   Playtesting:

- Enter Play mode and navigate the maze, testing movement, camera tracking, the timer, and collectibles.

Adjustments:

- Fine-tune maze layout, player speed, camera offset, and timer duration for a balanced gameplay experience.

Building a simple 3D maze game reinforces essential Unity skills, including level design, collision handling, player movement, camera controls, and UI elements like timers and scores. With this setup, you can expand the game further by adding additional objectives, visual effects, or more complex levels, creating a foundation for a fully-featured maze exploration experience.

Scripting with C# in Unity

Scripting is at the core of developing interactive and dynamic features in Unity, using C# as the primary programming language. Understanding Unity's scripting workflow, how scripts integrate as components within the GameObject system, and the lifecycle of scripts through MonoBehaviour methods is essential for creating functional, responsive gameplay. This chapter provides a comprehensive overview of these scripting fundamentals.

Unity's Scripting Workflow

Unity's scripting workflow revolves around creating C# scripts that control the behavior of GameObjects. A clear understanding of this workflow is key to organizing, testing, and implementing code in Unity.

1. Creating Scripts in Unity
Adding a Script to a GameObject:

- To create a new script, right-click in the **Project** window, select **Create > C# Script**, and give it a descriptive name. Alternatively, you can add a script directly to a GameObject by selecting it in the **Hierarchy** and choosing **Add Component > New Script** in the Inspector.

Organizing Scripts in the Project:

- For easier project management, store scripts in dedicated folders like **Scripts** or categorize them by function (e.g., **PlayerScripts**, **Ene-

myScripts). Unity automatically recompiles scripts each time you save changes, so efficient organization helps prevent confusion as the project grows.

Editing Scripts in an IDE:

- Open and edit scripts in an integrated development environment (IDE) like **Visual Studio** or **Rider**. Unity connects with these IDEs to provide code highlighting, debugging, and other useful features tailored to Unity's API.

Testing and Iteration:

- Unity's workflow emphasizes real-time testing. After making script changes, return to Unity, which automatically recompiles the scripts. You can then enter **Play Mode** to test the script's effects immediately.

Debugging:

- Use the **Console** window in Unity to catch errors and view logs. **Debug.Log** statements are commonly used to track variables, inspect object states, and verify code execution at various points in the script.

2. Script-Driven Development

In Unity, development is driven by scripts that enable interactivity. Scripts allow you to add behaviors, logic, and conditions to GameObjects, making it possible to create everything from player controls to enemy AI and complex UI systems.

Scripts as Modular Units:

- Unity uses a modular approach where each script typically handles a single responsibility or behavior. This modularity simplifies debugging, promotes reuse, and makes it easier to manage interactions between

GameObjects.

Scene-Based Testing:

- Scripts are often tested within specific scenes in Unity, allowing you to simulate and refine behaviors for specific game levels or interfaces. Testing in isolated scenes reduces the chance of unintended interactions affecting development.

Scripts as Components in Unity's GameObject System

Unity's **Component-Based Architecture** is designed to let you add modular behaviors to GameObjects by attaching scripts. In this system, scripts are treated as components that can be dynamically combined to produce complex behaviors.

1. GameObjects as Containers for Components

A **GameObject** in Unity is an empty entity by default, capable of holding multiple components, including scripts, colliders, renderers, and more.

Adding Components:

- Select a GameObject in the **Hierarchy** and choose **Add Component** in the Inspector to attach a script. Each attached component adds a specific functionality or behavior to the GameObject.
- You can attach multiple scripts to a single GameObject. For example, a player character might have scripts for movement, health, and inventory, each handling distinct aspects of player functionality.

Modifying Components:

- Unity allows you to modify component properties in real-time within the Inspector. For scripts, public variables defined in the script are exposed in the Inspector, enabling adjustments without needing to edit code directly.

- Modifying properties directly in the Inspector allows for quicker iterations, fine-tuning gameplay elements like movement speed, jump height, or enemy detection ranges.

Component Interaction:

- Scripts can access and control other components on the same GameObject or different GameObjects. For example, a player movement script may need to access the Rigidbody component to apply forces, or a health script may interact with a UI component to update the health display.

2. The Importance of Encapsulation in Script Components

Encapsulation in Unity scripts promotes modularity, keeping each script focused on a single responsibility. By using public and private variables effectively, you can protect certain variables while exposing only necessary properties in the Inspector.

- **Public Variables**: Public variables appear in the Inspector, allowing easy configuration of key settings, such as speed, health, or damage.
- **Private Variables with [SerializeField]**: Marking private variables with [SerializeField] makes them editable in the Inspector but keeps them inaccessible to other scripts, providing greater control over variable access.

3. Removing and Disabling Components

Components can be disabled or removed dynamically, allowing for conditional behaviors based on game state. For instance:

- **Disabling Components**: Temporarily disable a component, such as a movement script when the player is stunned, by toggling its enabled property.
- **Removing Components**: Certain effects, like destroying an enemy, may require removing or destroying specific components. Use De-

stroy(this); to remove a script or Destroy(gameObject); to remove the entire GameObject.

Understanding MonoBehaviour and Script Lifecycle Methods

MonoBehaviour is the base class from which all Unity scripts inherit. It provides access to Unity's built-in methods and game engine events, which define the lifecycle of a script. Understanding these lifecycle methods helps you create responsive and efficient behaviors in your games.

1. What is MonoBehaviour?
Inheritance from MonoBehaviour:

- All Unity scripts that attach to GameObjects derive from MonoBehaviour. This inheritance enables scripts to access MonoBehaviour methods like Start, Update, OnCollisionEnter, and more.
- MonoBehaviour also provides access to Unity's built-in properties and functions, such as transform, gameObject, and StartCoroutine, which facilitate gameplay development and interactions.

Importance of MonoBehaviour in Unity:

- By inheriting MonoBehaviour, a script can be attached to a GameObject, allowing it to participate in Unity's event system and lifecycle management.
- MonoBehaviour simplifies the coding process by providing pre-defined methods that handle initialization, frame updates, physics interactions, and other common game tasks.

2. Key MonoBehaviour Lifecycle Methods
Unity's MonoBehaviour lifecycle methods are called at specific points during the game, helping to organize code based on game events.
Awake():

- Called once when the script instance is initialized, regardless of whether the GameObject is active.
- Ideal for setting up references between components or initializing variables before the scene fully loads.

Start():

- Called on the frame when a script is enabled, before the first Update() method call.
- Often used to initialize variables, set up starting conditions, and trigger initial animations or sounds.

Update():

- Called once per frame, making it the main method for frame-based logic like player input, movement, and animations.
- Since Update() runs continuously, it's important to use it only for essential code to prevent performance issues.

FixedUpdate():

- Called at fixed intervals, regardless of frame rate, and is used primarily for physics-related calculations.
- Ideal for applying forces or checking physics-based collisions and interactions, as FixedUpdate runs in sync with Unity's physics engine.

LateUpdate():

- Called after Update() in each frame, making it suitable for operations that depend on other components' updates.
- Often used for camera-follow scripts, as it ensures that the camera positions itself correctly after the player moves.

3. Collision and Trigger Events

Collision and trigger events are part of MonoBehaviour and provide automatic methods for detecting physical interactions with other GameObjects.
OnCollisionEnter(), OnCollisionStay(), and OnCollisionExit():

- Handle physical collisions with GameObjects that have Collider components. These methods are useful for managing responses to impacts, such as taking damage or bouncing off obstacles.

OnTriggerEnter(), OnTriggerStay(), and OnTriggerExit():

- Trigger events work with colliders set as **Is Trigger** and allow objects to pass through each other while detecting interactions. Triggers are ideal for collecting items, entering zones, or activating events without physical collision.

4. Managing Game Flow with Coroutine Methods

Unity's coroutine system enables scripts to manage time-based events without blocking the main game thread.
Starting and Running Coroutines:

- Coroutines are methods that run in parallel to Update() and use yield return statements to pause execution until specified conditions are met.
- Coroutines are helpful for time-based actions, such as waiting a few seconds to respawn an enemy or triggering a sequence of actions in a cutscene.

Examples of Coroutine Usage:

- yield return new WaitForSeconds(3); pauses the coroutine for three seconds, while yield return null; waits until the next frame to continue execution.

Ending Coroutines:

- You can stop coroutines manually using StopCoroutine() or automatically when the GameObject is disabled or destroyed. This is important for managing performance and ensuring coroutines do not continue running when they are no longer needed.

Unity's scripting workflow, component-based architecture, and MonoBehaviour lifecycle methods provide a powerful framework for developing interactive and responsive gameplay. By understanding how scripts integrate as components, leverage lifecycle methods, and manage game flow through coroutines, you can create complex behaviors and interactions. These core concepts set the foundation for efficient, modular, and scalable game development in Unity.

Practical Scripting Techniques

Practical scripting techniques are critical for developing organized, efficient, and responsive gameplay. Managing game states, tracking player data, and effectively using collections like lists, arrays, and dictionaries allow you to store and access data dynamically, enabling smooth and functional game experiences.

Managing Game State and Player Data

In Unity, **game state** refers to various stages or conditions of the game, such as when the game is playing, paused, or game-over. Managing game state efficiently allows for smoother transitions, more control over gameplay, and a more immersive player experience.

1. Using Enums to Define Game States

Enums (enumerations) are helpful for defining and categorizing various game states. They make the code more readable and allow for easy state management within a switch-case structure.

```csharp
public enum GameState
{
    Menu,
    Playing,
    Paused,
    GameOver
}
```

2. Setting Up a GameManager to Handle Game State

A **GameManager** script serves as the central controller for tracking the game state. By defining a state and triggering specific actions depending on that state, the GameManager enables responsive control over different gameplay stages.

```csharp
using UnityEngine;

public class GameManager : MonoBehaviour
{
    public static GameManager Instance;
    public GameState currentState;

    void Awake()
    {
        if (Instance == null)
        {
            Instance = this;
            DontDestroyOnLoad(gameObject);
        }
        else
        {
            Destroy(gameObject);
        }
```

```
    }

    public void SetGameState(GameState newState)
    {
        currentState = newState;
        HandleGameStateChange();
    }

    private void HandleGameStateChange()
    {
        switch (currentState)
        {
            case GameState.Menu:
                // Show menu UI
                break;
            case GameState.Playing:
                // Start or resume gameplay
                Time.timeScale = 1; // Unpause game
                break;
            case GameState.Paused:
                // Pause the game
                Time.timeScale = 0; // Stop time
                break;
            case GameState.GameOver:
                // Trigger game-over actions
                break;
        }
    }
}
```

- **Singleton Pattern**: The GameManager uses a singleton pattern to ensure only one instance exists and is accessible from anywhere in the game.
- **Switch Statement**: Each case defines behaviors for specific game states, such as pausing or resuming gameplay.

3. Saving and Loading Player Data

SCRIPTING WITH C# IN UNITY

Unity provides several methods to save and retrieve player data, from PlayerPrefs to JSON files, depending on the complexity of the data.

Using PlayerPrefs for Simple Data:

- **PlayerPrefs** is ideal for basic data, such as player settings, high scores, or other simple statistics.

csharp

```csharp
public void SaveHighScore(int score)
{
    PlayerPrefs.SetInt("HighScore", score);
    PlayerPrefs.Save();
}

public int LoadHighScore()
{
    return PlayerPrefs.GetInt("HighScore", 0); // Returns 0 if no
    score is saved
}
```

Saving Complex Data with JSON:

- JSON is useful for storing more complex structures like inventories, character attributes, or level data.

csharp

```csharp
[System.Serializable]
public class PlayerData
{
    public int level;
    public int experience;
    public List<string> inventory;
}
```

```csharp
public void SavePlayerData(PlayerData data)
{
    string json = JsonUtility.ToJson(data);
    System.IO.File.WriteAllText(Application.persistentDataPath +
    "/playerData.json", json);
}

public PlayerData LoadPlayerData()
{
    string path = Application.persistentDataPath +
    "/playerData.json";
    if (System.IO.File.Exists(path))
    {
        string json = System.IO.File.ReadAllText(path);
        return JsonUtility.FromJson<PlayerData>(json);
    }
    return new PlayerData();
}
```

Using Scriptable Objects for In-Game Data:

- Scriptable Objects are assets that can hold game data and provide persistent access across scenes without runtime instantiation.

csharp

```csharp
[CreateAssetMenu(fileName = "NewPlayerStats", menuName = "Player
Stats")]
public class PlayerStats : ScriptableObject
{
    public int health;
    public int stamina;
}
```

- You can reference Scriptable Objects in multiple scripts, making them ideal for data shared across scenes, such as player stats or game settings.

Using Collections: Lists, Arrays, and Dictionaries

Collections enable you to store and manage related data in Unity. Arrays, lists, and dictionaries each have unique strengths suited to different use cases, from static data to dynamic, key-based data structures.

1. Arrays

Arrays are fixed-size collections that are efficient for storing elements when you know the number of items in advance.

```csharp
public class Waypoints : MonoBehaviour
{
    public Transform[] points;

    void Start()
    {
        for (int i = 0; i < points.Length; i++)
        {
            Debug.Log("Waypoint: " + points[i].position);
        }
    }
}
```

- **Fixed Size**: Arrays are ideal for static collections with a fixed number of elements.
- **Use Case**: Arrays are efficient for predefined data like level checkpoints or waypoints.

2. Lists

Lists are dynamic collections that can grow and shrink as needed. They're useful when working with elements that change frequently.

Using Lists:

- Declare lists using List<T>, where T represents the data type.

```csharp
using System.Collections.Generic;
using UnityEngine;

public class EnemyManager : MonoBehaviour
{
    public List<GameObject> enemies = new List<GameObject>();

    public void AddEnemy(GameObject enemy)
    {
        enemies.Add(enemy);
    }

    public void RemoveEnemy(GameObject enemy)
    {
        enemies.Remove(enemy);
    }

    void Update()
    {
        Debug.Log("Total enemies: " + enemies.Count);
    }
}
```

- **Add() and Remove()**: These methods let you add and remove elements dynamically.
- **Count**: Retrieves the number of items in the list.

Iterating Through Lists:

- Use foreach to iterate through lists easily.

```csharp

foreach (GameObject enemy in enemies)
{
    Debug.Log("Enemy Position: " + enemy.transform.position);
}
```

Use Case: Lists are ideal for data that changes frequently, like a player's inventory or active enemies in a level.

3. Dictionaries

Dictionaries store data as key-value pairs, enabling quick lookups and access by unique identifiers. They're especially useful for tracking elements that need to be accessed by a unique identifier, like inventory items or abilities mapped to controls.

Creating and Using Dictionaries:

- Declare a dictionary using Dictionary<TKey, TValue>, where TKey is the key type, and TValue is the value type.

```csharp

using System.Collections.Generic;

public class Inventory : MonoBehaviour
{
    public Dictionary<string, int> items = new Dictionary<string,
    int>();

    public void AddItem(string itemName, int quantity)
    {
        if (items.ContainsKey(itemName))
        {
            items[itemName] += quantity;
        }
```

```
        else
        {
            items[itemName] = quantity;
        }
    }

    public int GetItemQuantity(string itemName)
    {
        return items.ContainsKey(itemName) ? items[itemName] : 0;
    }
}
```

Explanation of the Dictionary Script:

- **ContainsKey()**: Checks if the key (item name) exists in the dictionary.
- **AddItem()**: Adds items or increases the quantity if the item already exists.
- **GetItemQuantity()**: Returns the quantity of the item or 0 if not found.

Accessing Dictionary Values:

- Retrieve values directly using their keys, making dictionaries efficient for complex inventories or skill systems.

Use Case: Dictionaries work best for data that requires unique identifiers and fast lookups, such as player inventory or mapping abilities to input controls.

Using practical scripting techniques in Unity allows for efficient management of game state, data persistence, and dynamic data manipulation through collections. Arrays, lists, and dictionaries provide diverse tools to structure and manage data, while methods for saving and loading player data ensure a seamless experience. Mastering these concepts equips you with the ability to manage complex game mechanics and optimize code for performance and scalability.

Debugging and Troubleshooting in Unity

Debugging is an essential skill for identifying and fixing issues that arise during game development. In Unity, debugging involves using the Console to identify errors and warnings, understanding common C# errors, and utilizing tools and best practices to diagnose and resolve issues efficiently.

Common C# Errors and How to Resolve Them

C# errors are common in Unity development, especially when dealing with syntax, logic, and runtime issues. Recognizing the cause of each error and knowing how to address it can save development time and prevent larger issues down the road.

1. Syntax Errors

Syntax errors occur when there are mistakes in the code structure, such as missing semicolons or incorrect brackets. These errors prevent the script from compiling and must be fixed before running the game.

Common Syntax Errors:

Missing Semicolon (;): Every C# statement must end with a semicolon.

csharp

```
int score = 10 // Error: Missing semicolon
```

Unmatched Braces or Parentheses: Opening { or (must be closed by } or).

csharp

```
if (score > 10 // Error: Missing closing parenthesis
{
Debug.Log("Score is greater than 10");
}
```

Resolving Syntax Errors:

Unity's Console will indicate the line number where the syntax error occurs. Review the line and check for common mistakes, such as missing characters or incorrect punctuation.

Use an IDE like Visual Studio, which highlights syntax errors in real-time and provides suggestions for correction.

2. NullReferenceException

A NullReferenceException occurs when the code tries to access an object or component that hasn't been initialized or assigned a value. This is one of the most common runtime errors in Unity.

Causes of NullReferenceException:

Attempting to use a GameObject or component that hasn't been assigned.

Forgetting to assign a reference in the Inspector or through code.

Example and Solution:

csharp

```
public GameObject player;

void Start()
    {
    player.GetComponent<Rigidbody>().AddForce(Vector3.up * 10); // Error if 'player' is not assigned
    }
```

Solution: Ensure player is assigned in the Inspector or initialize it in the code.

csharp

```
void Start()
    {
    if (player != null)
    {
    player.GetComponent<Rigidbody>().AddForce(Vector3.up * 10);
    }
    else
    {
    Debug.LogError("Player GameObject is not assigned!");
    }
    }
```

3. IndexOutOfRangeException

An IndexOutOfRangeException occurs when the code tries to access an element in an array or list that doesn't exist.

Causes of IndexOutOfRangeException:

Attempting to access an index that's beyond the range of an array or list.

Looping through an array or list with an incorrect index value.

Example and Solution:

csharp

```
int[] scores = new int[3] {10, 20, 30};
    Debug.Log(scores[3]); // Error: Index out of range
    Solution: Ensure the index is within the valid range.
```

csharp

```
for (int i = 0; i < scores.Length; i++)
    {
    Debug.Log(scores[i]);
    }
```

4. Type Mismatch Errors

Type mismatch errors occur when assigning incompatible types, such as trying to assign a float to an int variable without casting.

Example and Solution:

csharp

```
int score = 10.5f; // Error: Cannot convert float to int
    Solution: Convert the value to the appropriate type using casting.
    csharp
```

```
int score = (int)10.5f;
```

5. ArgumentOutOfRangeException

An ArgumentOutOfRangeException occurs when accessing a list or array with an index outside the bounds of the collection.

Cause and Solution:

csharp

List<string> names = new List<string> { "Alice", "Bob" };
Debug.Log(names[2]); // Error: Index is out of range

Ensure the index is within bounds, or check Count before accessing.

6. MissingReferenceException

A MissingReferenceException often occurs when trying to access a destroyed GameObject or component.

Cause:

This typically happens if a GameObject is destroyed but still referenced in code.

Solution:

Check for null references before accessing GameObjects or components. Use conditional checks:

csharp

```
if (enemy != null)
{
enemy.TakeDamage(10);
}
```

Using Unity's Console for Debugging

Unity's Console is a powerful tool for identifying and resolving errors, warnings, and general information messages within the editor.

1. Accessing and Understanding Console Messages

Types of Console Messages:

Error (Red): Indicates a critical issue that prevents code from running correctly.

Warning (Yellow): Highlights potential issues that don't stop the code but may cause problems.

Log (White): General information for tracking code behavior.

Using Debug.Log, Debug.LogWarning, and Debug.LogError:

Debug.Log provides runtime feedback, allowing you to inspect variables and check whether certain conditions are met.

csharp

```
int score = 100;
Debug.Log("Player Score: " + score);
```

Debug.LogWarning and Debug.LogError are useful for highlighting issues. For example, if a certain value exceeds an expected range, Debug.LogWarning can alert you.

csharp

```
if (score < 0)
{
Debug.LogWarning("Score is below zero!");
}
```

Debug.LogError signals critical problems:

csharp

```
if (health <= 0)
{
Debug.LogError("Player has died.");
}
```

2. Filtering and Searching in the Console

The Console provides options to filter specific message types or search for keywords. This helps streamline the debugging process, especially in complex projects with numerous logs.

Filtering: Toggle filters at the top of the Console to show or hide specific messages (e.g., only Errors).

Search Bar: Use the search bar to find specific log messages by keyword or variable names.

3. Double-Clicking Console Messages for Quick Navigation

Click on an error or warning message in the Console to jump directly to the relevant line in the script. This feature accelerates the troubleshooting process by taking you directly to the issue in the code.

4. Using Breakpoints and Stepping Through Code

For more complex debugging, you can use an IDE like Visual Studio with Unity's Attach to Unity feature, which allows breakpoints and stepping through code line by line.

Setting Breakpoints:

Place breakpoints in Visual Studio by clicking next to the line number. This pauses execution when the line is reached.

While debugging, inspect variable values and step through code to see how execution flows.

Attaching to Unity:

Select Attach to Unity in Visual Studio to start debugging. When Unity reaches a breakpoint, it will pause, allowing you to inspect variables and step through the code.

Using Step Over, Step Into, and Step Out:

Step Over moves to the next line in the same function.

Step Into goes into any functions called on the current line.

Step Out exits the current function and returns to the caller.

Best Practices for Debugging

Use Debug.Log Sparingly:

While Debug.Log is helpful, excessive logging can clutter the Console and slow performance, especially in intensive scripts. Use logs strategically to trace key values and events.

Encapsulate Debug Code with Conditional Compilation:

Use #if UNITY_EDITOR directives to ensure that debug logs only run in the editor, preventing performance issues in the final build.

csharp

#if UNITY_EDITOR

Debug.Log("Player Health: " + health);

#endif

Comment and Document Code:

Detailed comments make it easier to understand code when troubleshooting, especially in collaborative projects or complex functions.

Simplify Complex Functions for Easier Debugging:

Break down long functions into smaller methods for readability and ease of debugging. Smaller functions are easier to test independently.

Debugging and troubleshooting are critical components of game development in Unity. By understanding common C# errors, utilizing Unity's Console effectively, and following best practices, you can streamline the development process, resolve issues efficiently, and deliver a more stable, polished game. Mastering these techniques helps you anticipate and address potential problems, making debugging less daunting and ensuring smoother, more consistent gameplay.

Advanced Unity Features for Beginners

Unity's UI (User Interface) system provides tools to create interactive, visually appealing interfaces that enhance player experience. This chapter will cover the essentials of Unity's UI system, including its components and workflow, and will guide you through creating menus, buttons, and interactive UI elements, laying a solid foundation for developing engaging interfaces.

Unity UI Essentials

The Unity UI system is built to create dynamic and interactive screens, menus, and in-game elements. It's a flexible toolset that works alongside other Unity features, enabling developers to build interfaces ranging from simple score displays to complex inventories.

1. Overview of the Unity UI System

Unity's UI system primarily operates through **Canvas** and **RectTransform** components, which form the foundation for all UI elements.

Canvas:

- The Canvas is the root component for UI elements, responsible for organizing and rendering all UI components in a scene. Every UI element, such as buttons, images, or text, must be a child of a Canvas to appear on the screen.
- **Render Modes**:
- **Screen Space - Overlay**: The UI renders on top of the game, covering

the entire screen.

- **Screen Space - Camera**: The UI is tied to a specific camera, giving flexibility for camera-based effects.
- **World Space**: The UI becomes a 3D object in the scene, suitable for in-world displays or interfaces on objects.

RectTransform:

- The **RectTransform** is a special Transform component for UI elements. It defines the element's position, size, and anchor within the Canvas.
- **Anchors and Pivot Points**:
- Anchors define the position relative to the Canvas edges or a parent UI element. By setting anchors, you can make UI elements responsive to different screen sizes.
- The pivot point is the element's center of rotation and scaling, which can be adjusted to customize positioning behavior.

UI Elements:

- Unity provides a range of built-in UI elements, including **Text, Image, Button, Slider, Toggle**, and **Input Field**. Each element is customizable and supports interactivity, making it easy to create functional interfaces.

Introduction to Unity's UI System

Understanding the core components of Unity's UI system is essential for developing responsive and interactive interfaces. Unity's UI system is part of the **UnityEngine.UI** namespace, which contains all necessary classes and components for creating UIs.

1. Setting Up the Canvas

To begin creating UI elements, you need a Canvas in the scene.
Adding a Canvas:

- Go to **GameObject > UI > Canvas**. Unity automatically creates a Canvas GameObject along with an **EventSystem**, which handles input and interactivity.
- The Canvas can be adjusted in the **Inspector** to use different render modes, depending on the type of UI required.

Understanding Canvas Scaler:

- The **Canvas Scaler** component adjusts the scale of UI elements based on screen size. By setting the **UI Scale Mode** to **Scale with Screen Size**, you can ensure that UI elements adapt to different resolutions.
- **Reference Resolution**: Sets the base resolution for scaling. For example, if set to 1920x1080, the UI scales proportionally to maintain the same look across screens.

2. Working with the RectTransform

The RectTransform allows precise control over the layout and positioning of UI elements. Each RectTransform provides controls for **position, scale, pivot**, and **anchoring**.

Anchoring for Responsive Design:

- Anchors are crucial for creating responsive UIs that adjust to different screen sizes and orientations.
- Set anchors in the **RectTransform** to dynamically position UI elements. For example, setting both anchors to the screen's bottom-right corner keeps a UI element, like a "Settings" button, consistently in that position across resolutions.

Pivot and Positioning:

- The pivot point determines the element's center point for transformations (scaling, rotation). Adjusting the pivot enables precise control over how elements align and move.

- Use the **Position** fields in the RectTransform to place elements within the Canvas. Positions can be absolute or relative to the anchors for flexible positioning.

Creating Menus, Buttons, and Interactive UI Elements

Menus and buttons are fundamental components for player interaction in most games, serving as entry points to settings, instructions, or gameplay options.

1. Creating a Basic Menu

Menus are often the first UI elements players encounter, so designing them clearly and interactively is important. Here's how to create a main menu with buttons for common functions, such as Start, Settings, and Quit.

Creating Background Panels:

- Go to **GameObject > UI > Panel** to add a background panel to the Canvas. The panel's **Image** component allows you to set a color or background image, enhancing the menu's visual appeal.
- Adjust the panel's RectTransform to fit the Canvas or specific portions of the screen, depending on your design.

Adding Menu Buttons:

- Go to **GameObject > UI > Button** to create a button. Rename it appropriately (e.g., StartButton) and place it within the background panel.
- Customize the button's **Text** component to change the label to "Start" or other desired text.

Styling Buttons:

- Use the **Image** component to set button colors, gradients, or images for different states (Normal, Highlighted, Pressed).

- Adjust the **Font** and **Text Color** in the **Text** component for readability and theme consistency.

2. Adding Button Functionality

To make buttons functional, add scripts to control their behavior when clicked. Unity's UI system allows you to link button clicks to specific methods, creating interactive elements quickly.

Creating a UI Manager Script:

- Create a new script named UIManager to handle button actions.

```csharp
using UnityEngine;
using UnityEngine.SceneManagement;

public class UIManager : MonoBehaviour
{
    public void StartGame()
    {
        SceneManager.LoadScene("GameScene");
// Replace "GameScene" with your scene name
    }

    public void OpenSettings()
    {
        // Display the settings menu
        Debug.Log("Settings Opened");
    }

    public void QuitGame()
    {
        Application.Quit();
        Debug.Log("Game Quit");
    }
}
```

Linking Buttons to Functions:

- Select the StartButton in the Hierarchy and scroll to the **On Click** section in the Button component.
- Click + to add an action, assign the **UIManager** GameObject, and select the StartGame method.
- Repeat this process for other buttons, linking each to their respective functions, like OpenSettings and QuitGame.

Testing Button Interactions:

- Enter Play mode to test the button interactions. Click each button to ensure they trigger the assigned functions and navigate as expected.

3. Adding Interactive Elements: Sliders, Toggles, and Input Fields
In addition to buttons, Unity's UI system provides interactive elements such as **Sliders, Toggles**, and **Input Fields** for collecting and displaying player input.

Creating a Slider for Volume Control:

- Go to **GameObject > UI > Slider** to add a slider. Sliders are useful for adjustable settings, like volume or brightness.
- Create a method in the UIManager script to link the slider value to an audio setting.

```csharp
using UnityEngine;
using UnityEngine.UI;

public class UIManager : MonoBehaviour
{
    public Slider volumeSlider;
```

```
void Start()
{
    volumeSlider.onValueChanged.AddListener(AdjustVolume);
}

public void AdjustVolume(float volume)
{
    AudioListener.volume = volume;
}
}
```

Adding Toggle Options:

- Toggling options are helpful for settings such as enabling/disabling music, graphics quality, or other binary choices.
- Go to **GameObject > UI > Toggle** to add a toggle. Customize the label text and link it to a function in UIManager.

```csharp
csharp

public void ToggleMusic(bool isEnabled)
{
    // Logic to enable/disable music
    Debug.Log("Music Enabled: " + isEnabled);
}
```

Using Input Fields for Text Entry:

- **Input Fields** are useful for name entry, search functions, or any text input. Go to **GameObject > UI > Input Field** to create an input field.
- Link the input field to a function to capture the text entered by the player.

```csharp
public InputField nameInput;

public void SavePlayerName()
{
    string playerName = nameInput.text;
    Debug.Log("Player Name: " + playerName);
}
```

4. Organizing UI Elements with Layout Groups

Unity provides **Layout Groups** to arrange UI elements systematically, such as vertical or horizontal layouts.

Adding a Vertical Layout Group:

- Select the panel or Canvas and add a **Vertical Layout Group** from the Inspector to align elements vertically (e.g., Start, Settings, Quit buttons).
- The Layout Group automatically spaces and aligns elements, making it easy to design consistent UI structures.

Spacing and Padding:

- Adjust **Spacing** to control the distance between items and **Padding** to add space around the edges, enhancing readability and visual appeal

Unity's UI system is a versatile toolset for creating interactive, user-friendly interfaces that enhance gameplay. By mastering Canvas settings, RectTransforms, and interactive elements like buttons, sliders, and input fields, you can develop responsive UIs tailored to various gameplay needs. Practicing these techniques will enable you to design polished, intuitive menus and interfaces that elevate the player experience.

Sound and Music in Unity

Sound and music play a crucial role in creating immersive and engaging experiences in games. Unity offers robust tools for integrating audio, allowing developers to add sound effects, background music, and interactive audio cues. This section will cover the essentials of adding sound in Unity, implementing sound controls, and creating triggers for dynamic audio behavior.

Adding Sound Effects and Background Music

In Unity, sound can be added to scenes in the form of audio files (e.g., .wav, .mp3) and controlled through components like **AudioSource** and **AudioListener**. With these components, you can play background music, trigger sound effects, and manage audio settings.

1. Preparing Audio Files for Unity

Before integrating sound, make sure your audio files are optimized and imported correctly:

Importing Audio Files:

- Drag audio files directly into the **Assets** folder. Unity will automatically recognize and convert them for use in the project.
- Organize audio files in folders, such as **Music** and **SFX**, to maintain a clean project structure.

Audio File Settings:

- Select an audio file in the Assets folder to view its **Inspector** settings.
- Adjust the **Load Type** to Streaming for longer files (e.g., background music) or Decompress on Load for short sound effects to optimize memory use.
- Set the **Compression Format** to balance quality and performance based on the type of audio and platform requirements.

2. Using AudioSource Components

An **AudioSource** component plays audio clips attached to GameObjects. You can configure the AudioSource to play sounds, loop background music, and adjust settings like volume and pitch.

Adding an AudioSource:

- Select the GameObject that will play the sound (e.g., Main Camera for background music or Player for sound effects).
- Go to **Add Component > Audio > AudioSource** to add the AudioSource component.

Configuring AudioSource Settings:

- **AudioClip**: Assign the audio file to play. Drag and drop an audio clip from the Assets folder into the AudioClip field in the AudioSource.
- **Loop**: Enable this option to loop the audio clip, useful for background music that should repeat continuously.
- **Play On Awake**: When enabled, the audio plays automatically when the scene starts. Typically used for background music or ambient sounds.
- **Volume and Pitch**: Adjust the volume and pitch for each audio source. You can manipulate these settings dynamically through scripts for effects like fading or pitch shifting.

Playing Sounds Through Scripts:

- Use scripts to control when sounds play, especially for non-looping sound effects triggered by specific events.

```csharp

using UnityEngine;
```

```
public class AudioManager : MonoBehaviour
{
    public AudioSource soundEffectSource;
    public AudioClip jumpSound;

    public void PlayJumpSound()
    {
        soundEffectSource.PlayOneShot(jumpSound);
    }
}
```

- **PlayOneShot**: Plays a sound without interrupting the current clip. Useful for short sound effects like gunshots or button clicks.

Implementing Background Music

Background music enhances the game's atmosphere, setting the tone and engaging players. To add background music, use an AudioSource on a persistent GameObject.

Setting Up Background Music:

- Create an empty GameObject called MusicPlayer and add an **AudioSource** component.
- Assign the background music clip to the AudioSource's **AudioClip** field.
- Enable **Loop** to ensure the music repeats.

Using the Singleton Pattern for Persistent Music:

- For consistent background music across multiple scenes, make the MusicPlayer a persistent GameObject.

```csharp

using UnityEngine;

public class MusicPlayer : MonoBehaviour
{
    private static MusicPlayer instance;

    void Awake()
    {
        if (instance == null)
        {
            instance = this;
            DontDestroyOnLoad(gameObject);
        }
        else
        {
            Destroy(gameObject);
        }
    }
}
```

Controlling Music Playback in Scripts:

- Use methods like **Play**, **Pause**, and **Stop** to control background music, such as pausing during game-over scenes or transitioning to new music.

```csharp

public void StopMusic()
{
    GetComponent<AudioSource>().Stop();
}
```

Implementing Sound Controls and Triggers

Sound controls and triggers add interactivity to audio, allowing sound to respond to player actions and environmental changes dynamically.

1. Adding Volume Controls

Volume controls are common in game settings, allowing players to adjust music and sound effect levels. To achieve this, use sliders that control AudioSource volume levels.

Creating a Volume Slider:

- Go to **GameObject > UI > Slider** to create a volume slider in the UI.
- Name the slider (e.g., MusicVolumeSlider) and position it within the settings menu.

Linking the Slider to Volume Control:

- Create a UIManager script to handle the slider's value and adjust the AudioSource volume accordingly.

```csharp
using UnityEngine;
using UnityEngine.UI;

public class UIManager : MonoBehaviour
{
    public Slider musicVolumeSlider;
    public AudioSource musicSource;

    void Start()
    {
        musicVolumeSlider.onValueChanged
.AddListener(AdjustMusicVolume);
    }

    public void AdjustMusicVolume(float volume)
    {
        musicSource.volume = volume;
    }
```

```
}
```

- The **AdjustMusicVolume** method links the slider's value to the AudioSource's volume, allowing players to adjust the background music volume in real-time.

2. Using Audio Triggers

Triggers enable sounds to play based on player interactions, such as entering specific areas or performing actions like jumping or collecting items.

Setting Up a Trigger Collider:

- Create an empty GameObject and add a **Box Collider** component.
- Enable **Is Trigger** to allow the collider to detect entry without obstructing movement.

Creating an Audio Trigger Script

An Audio Trigger script detects when the player enters the trigger area and plays a sound.

```csharp
using UnityEngine;

public class AudioTrigger : MonoBehaviour
{
    public AudioSource audioSource;

    void OnTriggerEnter(Collider other)
    {
        if (other.CompareTag("Player"))
        {
            audioSource.Play();
        }
```

```
        }
}
```

- Attach the script to the trigger collider and assign an AudioSource with the desired sound effect.
- When the player enters the trigger area, the **OnTriggerEnter** method plays the sound.

Using Trigger Events for Environmental Sounds:

- Triggers can also activate sounds for environmental elements, like ambient music in different zones, footsteps on different surfaces, or nearby hazards.

```csharp
public AudioClip forestAmbience;
public AudioClip caveAmbience;

public void OnTriggerEnter(Collider other)
{
    if (other.CompareTag("ForestZone"))
    {
        audioSource.clip = forestAmbience;
        audioSource.Play();
    }
    else if (other.CompareTag("CaveZone"))
    {
        audioSource.clip = caveAmbience;
        audioSource.Play();
    }
}
```

3. Implementing 3D Sound Effects for Realism

Unity's AudioSource component allows you to create spatial audio effects by adjusting 3D sound settings. This can add realism, as sounds will change volume and panning based on the player's position relative to the source.

Enabling 3D Sound:

- Select the AudioSource component and set **Spatial Blend** to 3D. The sound will now behave spatially in the game world.

Configuring 3D Sound Settings:

- **Max Distance:** Sets the maximum distance at which the sound can be heard.
- **Rolloff Mode:** Determines how sound diminishes over distance. **Linear** rolloff decreases sound in a straight line from the source, while **Logarithmic** rolloff provides a more realistic fade.

Applying 3D Sound for Positional Effects:

- Attach 3D sound effects to dynamic objects, like moving enemies or environmental hazards. As the player moves closer or farther from the sound source, the volume and panning will change, enhancing immersion.

Integrating sound and music into Unity games involves more than just adding background tracks and sound effects. With tools like AudioSource, AudioListener, and trigger-based sound controls, you can create immersive, responsive audio experiences that adapt to player actions and the environment. Mastering these audio tools enhances your game's atmosphere and brings its world to life, providing players with a richer, more engaging experience.

Simple AI for Game Elements

AI in games adds dynamism and challenge, allowing non-player characters (NPCs) to interact meaningfully with the player and their environment. Unity's built-in **NavMesh** system provides pathfinding tools for AI agents, enabling them to navigate through complex scenes. We'll cover the basics of setting up NavMesh, adding NavMeshAgents, and scripting simple AI behaviors such as patrolling, chasing, and attacking.

Introduction to Pathfinding with NavMesh

Pathfinding is essential for any game involving NPCs that need to navigate a scene. Unity's NavMesh system enables developers to create walkable surfaces that AI characters can traverse, moving intelligently around obstacles and reaching designated targets.

1. Setting Up NavMesh in Unity
Creating a NavMesh:

- Open **Window > AI > Navigation** to access Unity's Navigation panel, which enables you to define the walkable areas in your scene.
- Go to the **Bake** tab and adjust parameters such as **Agent Radius**, **Agent Height**, and **Max Slope** to match the dimensions and movement capabilities of your AI agents.
- Click **Bake** to generate the NavMesh. Unity will display walkable areas in blue, showing where the NPCs can navigate.

Key NavMesh Parameters:

- **Agent Radius**: Controls the width of the path that the AI agent requires. Increasing the radius avoids narrow areas, while a smaller radius allows the agent to pass through tighter spaces.
- **Agent Height**: Ensures that only areas where the agent fits vertically are walkable.
- **Step Height**: Defines the maximum height difference the AI can step over, useful for varied terrains.

Adding NavMesh Obstacles:

- Use **NavMesh Obstacles** on objects that NPCs should avoid, such as walls or large objects. This dynamically modifies the path, helping NPCs navigate around these obstacles.

2. Adding and Configuring NavMeshAgents

A **NavMeshAgent** component enables GameObjects to move along the NavMesh.

Adding a NavMeshAgent:

- Select the GameObject representing your NPC or enemy and go to **Add Component > Navigation > NavMeshAgent**.
- Adjust properties such as **Speed** (how fast the agent moves), **Angular Speed** (how quickly the agent turns), and **Stopping Distance** (how close the agent stops to its destination).

Basic Movement with NavMeshAgent:

- Control the NavMeshAgent's movement by setting a destination in code. The agent will automatically navigate the NavMesh to reach this point.

```csharp
using UnityEngine;
using UnityEngine.AI;

public class EnemyAI : MonoBehaviour
{
    public Transform target; // Player or a point of interest
    private NavMeshAgent agent;

    void Start()
```

```
    {
        agent = GetComponent<NavMeshAgent>();
        agent.SetDestination(target.position);
    }

    void Update()
    {
        agent.SetDestination(target.position);
// Continuously update destination for dynamic movement
    }
}
```

Creating Basic Enemy Behavior Scripts

Basic enemy behaviors like patrolling, chasing, and attacking make the game more interactive and engaging. Combining NavMesh with simple scripting allows you to create a wide range of AI behaviors, including patrolling predetermined paths, detecting and chasing players, and triggering attacks when in range.

1. Implementing Patrol Behavior

Patrolling is a fundamental AI behavior where the NPC follows a set of waypoints in a loop, mimicking guard-like behavior. This gives players predictable movement patterns to interact with.

Setting Up Patrol Waypoints:

- Add empty GameObjects to the scene to represent patrol points and place them along the desired patrol route.
- Create an array to store these waypoints in the script, allowing the agent to move between them.

Patrol Script Implementation:

- Define a patrol script where the NPC moves to each waypoint and, upon reaching it, proceeds to the next one.

```csharp
using UnityEngine;
using UnityEngine.AI;

public class EnemyPatrol : MonoBehaviour
{
    public Transform[] waypoints;
    private NavMeshAgent agent;
    private int currentWaypointIndex = 0;

    void Start()
    {
        agent = GetComponent<NavMeshAgent>();
        MoveToNextWaypoint();
    }

    void MoveToNextWaypoint()
    {
        if (waypoints.Length == 0)
            return;

        agent.SetDestination(waypoints
[currentWaypointIndex].position);
    }

    void Update()
    {
        if (agent.remainingDistance
 < 0.5f && !agent.pathPending)
        {
            currentWaypointIndex =
(currentWaypointIndex + 1) % waypoints.Length;
            MoveToNextWaypoint();
        }
    }
}
```

- This script instructs the agent to move to each waypoint in order, looping back to the first waypoint after reaching the last.

2. Implementing Chasing Behavior

Chasing behavior allows the enemy to detect the player within a certain range and follow them. This adds tension and urgency to gameplay, making it critical for players to avoid or defend against the enemy.

Detecting the Player's Presence:

- Use a **Sphere Collider** set as a trigger around the NPC to define its detection range. When the player enters this range, the NPC initiates the chase.

```csharp
void OnTriggerEnter(Collider other)
{
    if (other.CompareTag("Player"))
    {
        agent.SetDestination(other.transform.position);
    }
}

void OnTriggerStay(Collider other)
{
    if (other.CompareTag("Player"))
    {
        agent.SetDestination(other.
transform.position); // Continuously update to follow player
    }
}

void OnTriggerExit(Collider other)
{
    if (other.CompareTag("Player"))
    {
```

```
        MoveToNextWaypoint(); // Resume
patrolling if player leaves detection range
    }
}
```

Adjusting Chase Speed and Reactivity:

- Increase the **Speed** property of the NavMeshAgent while in chase mode to create a sense of urgency and challenge for the player.

```csharp
private float normalSpeed = 3.5f;
private float chaseSpeed = 5.5f;

void OnTriggerEnter(Collider other)
{
    if (other.CompareTag("Player"))
    {
        agent.speed = chaseSpeed;
        agent.SetDestination(other.transform.position);
    }
}

void OnTriggerExit(Collider other)
{
    agent.speed = normalSpeed;
// Revert to normal speed after player leaves
    MoveToNextWaypoint();
}
```

3. Implementing Attack Behavior

Attacking behavior enables the enemy to strike the player when close enough, adding further depth to the AI. This often includes stopping movement and triggering attack animations or sounds.

Defining Attack Range:

- Set a small radius around the NPC to define when they will initiate an attack. When the player is within this range, the NPC stops moving and engages in an attack.

Basic Attack Logic:

- Stop the NavMeshAgent when the player is within attack range and initiate an attack cooldown to avoid repeated attacks.

```csharp
private float attackRange = 1.5f;
private bool isAttacking = false;

void Update()
{
    float distanceToPlayer = Vector3.
Distance(transform.position, player.position);

    if (distanceToPlayer <= attackRange && !isAttacking)
    {
        StartCoroutine(AttackPlayer());
    }
    else if (distanceToPlayer > attackRange && isAttacking)
    {
        agent.SetDestination(player.position);
// Resume chasing if player moves away
        isAttacking = false;
    }
}

private IEnumerator AttackPlayer()
{
    isAttacking = true;
    agent.isStopped = true;

    // Placeholder attack logic, such as reducing player health
```

```
    Debug.Log("Attacking Player!");

    yield return new WaitForSeconds(1.0f);
  // Cooldown between attacks
    agent.isStopped = false;
    isAttacking = false;
}
```

Explanation of Attack Behavior:

- **Attack Range**: Defines how close the player must be for the NPC to engage in an attack.
- **Coroutine AttackPlayer**: Starts a cooldown after each attack, pausing further attacks for a set duration to balance gameplay.

Adding Attack Animations and Sounds:

- Enhance the attack with animations and sound effects by triggering an **Animator** and **AudioSource** component within the AttackPlayer coroutine.

Creating simple AI for game elements in Unity involves combining pathfinding through NavMesh with scripted behaviors like patrolling, chasing, and attacking. By mastering these techniques, you can develop interactive and responsive NPCs that enrich gameplay, challenge players, and contribute to a dynamic game environment. These foundational AI behaviors lay the groundwork for developing more complex interactions, increasing engagement, and providing a more immersive experience for players.

Creating a Save System for Player Progress

A save system is essential in games that track player achievements, progress, or settings across sessions. By saving and loading player data, you

205

allow players to continue from where they left off. In Unity, creating a save system can be accomplished using a combination of file I/O, serialization, and persistent data storage techniques.

Saving and Loading Data in Unity

Unity provides multiple methods to save and load data, including **Player-Prefs** for simple data, **JSON Serialization** for structured data, and **binary files** for more secure storage. Each method has specific use cases based on the type of data being saved and the level of persistence required.

1. Using PlayerPrefs for Basic Data

PlayerPrefs is a built-in Unity class that saves small pieces of data, such as player preferences or settings, in the form of key-value pairs. It's ideal for simple, persistent data, like high scores or sound volume levels.

Saving Data with PlayerPrefs:

• PlayerPrefs allows you to save integers, floats, and strings with ease.

```csharp
public void SaveHighScore(int score)
{
    PlayerPrefs.SetInt("HighScore", score);
    PlayerPrefs.Save();
  // Saves all modified preferences to disk
}
```

Loading Data with PlayerPrefs:

• Retrieve saved data using the associated key. If the key doesn't exist, a default value is returned.

```csharp
public int LoadHighScore()
{
    return PlayerPrefs.GetInt
("HighScore", 0); // Default value is 0
}
```

Clearing Data with PlayerPrefs:

- For resetting data, PlayerPrefs offers methods to delete specific keys or clear all saved data.

```csharp
public void ResetHighScore()
{
    PlayerPrefs.DeleteKey("HighScore");
}
```

Use Case: PlayerPrefs is ideal for small, non-sensitive data like settings or scores but is limited by data size and structure.

JSON Serialization for Structured Data

JSON (JavaScript Object Notation) is a flexible, human-readable format suitable for saving complex data structures, such as player inventories, game progress, or configuration files. Unity's **JsonUtility** class provides easy methods for serializing and deserializing data to and from JSON, allowing structured data to be saved as a JSON string and stored on disk.

1. Defining a Data Model

First, create a **PlayerData** class to represent the information you want to save, such as level, health, experience, or inventory items.

csharp

```
[System.Serializable]
public class PlayerData
{
    public int level;
    public int health;
    public int experience;
    public List<string> inventory;
}
```

2. Saving Data with JSON Serialization

Serialize the PlayerData instance to JSON format and save it to a file. The Application.persistentDataPath provides a reliable path for storing data across platforms.

csharp

```
using System.IO;
using UnityEngine;

public class SaveSystem : MonoBehaviour
{
    public void SavePlayerData(PlayerData data)
    {
        string json = JsonUtility.ToJson(data);
// Serialize data to JSON
        File.WriteAllText(Application.persistentDataPath +
        "/playerData.json", json); // Save JSON to file
    }
}
```

3. Loading Data with JSON Deserialization

When loading data, read the JSON file, then deserialize the content back into a PlayerData object.

```csharp
csharp

public PlayerData LoadPlayerData()
{
    string path = Application.persistentDataPath +
    "/playerData.json";
    if (File.Exists(path))
    {
        string json = File.ReadAllText
(path); // Read JSON file
        return JsonUtility.FromJson
<PlayerData>(json); // Deserialize
 JSON to PlayerData object
    }
    else
    {
        Debug.LogWarning("Save file not found!");
        return new PlayerData();
// Return a new PlayerData object if no save exists
    }
}
```

Use Case: JSON serialization is excellent for structured data, such as save states, character progress, or game configurations. It's flexible, easily readable, and widely supported.

Simple File I/O and Data Persistence Techniques

File I/O (Input/Output) operations allow reading from and writing to files, enabling data persistence across game sessions. Unity supports various file handling methods, which we can combine with serialization to store data on disk.

1. Using Binary Serialization for Secure Data

Binary serialization converts data into a compact, non-human-readable format, making it more secure than plain text or JSON. Unity's BinaryFormatter can be used to serialize data into binary files, which are more difficult to edit, thus enhancing data integrity.

Note: Unity discourages using BinaryFormatter directly due to security concerns, especially with untrusted data. For production projects, consider safer alternatives or secure binary formats.

Creating a Serializable Data Class:

```csharp
[System.Serializable]
public class PlayerData
{
    public int level;
    public int health;
    public int experience;
}
```

Saving Data with Binary Serialization:

```csharp
using System.IO;
using System.Runtime.Serialization.Formatters.Binary;
using UnityEngine;

public class BinarySaveSystem : MonoBehaviour
{
    public void SaveData(PlayerData data)
    {
        BinaryFormatter formatter = new BinaryFormatter();
        string path = Application.persistentDataPath +
        "/playerData.dat";
        using (FileStream fileStream = new FileStream(path,
        FileMode.Create))
        {
            formatter.Serialize(fileStream, data);
        }
    }
}
```

Loading Data with Binary Deserialization:

210

```csharp
public PlayerData LoadData()
{
    string path = Application.persistentDataPath +
"/playerData.dat";
    if (File.Exists(path))
    {
        BinaryFormatter formatter =
new BinaryFormatter();
        using (FileStream fileStream =
new FileStream(path, FileMode.Open))
        {
            return (PlayerData)formatter.
Deserialize(fileStream);
        }
    }
    else
    {
        Debug.LogWarning("Save file not found");
        return new PlayerData();
    }
}
```

Use Case: Binary serialization is ideal for more secure and compact storage, suitable for larger datasets where human readability isn't necessary, such as encrypted save files or sensitive data.

Implementing a Save and Load System with Multiple Save Slots

Many games allow players to save and load from multiple slots, which is particularly useful for games with branching paths or different playstyles. Implementing multiple save slots requires managing file naming conventions and file I/O operations.

1. Setting Up Save Slots
Defining Slot-Specific File Names:

- Use slot-specific file names or directories, such as playerData_slot1.json or slot1/playerData.json.

Saving to a Specified Slot:

- Modify the save function to accept a slot number, which appends a suffix to the filename for each slot.

```csharp
public void SaveToSlot(PlayerData data, int slot)
{
    string json = JsonUtility.ToJson(data);
    File.WriteAllText(Application.persistentDataPath +
    $"/playerData_slot{slot}.json", json);
}
```

Loading from a Specified Slot:

- The load function reads from the slot-specific file based on the provided slot number.

```csharp
public PlayerData LoadFromSlot(int slot)
{
    string path = Application.persistentDataPath +
    $"/playerData_slot{slot}.json";
    if (File.Exists(path))
    {
        string json = File.ReadAllText(path);
        return JsonUtility.FromJson<PlayerData>(json);
    }
    else
    {
```

```
        Debug.LogWarning
("Save file not found for slot " + slot);
        return new PlayerData();
    }
}
```

Listing Available Save Slots:

- To display available save slots in a menu, you can use Directory.GetFiles() to check for existing save files.

```csharp
public int[] GetAvailableSlots()
{
    string[] files =
    Directory.GetFiles(Application.persistentDataPath,
    "playerData_slot*.json");
    return files.Select(f =>
    int.Parse(Path.GetFileNameWithoutExtension
(f).Split('_')[1])).ToArray();
}
```

Handling Data Persistence Across Sessions
Unity offers several options for data persistence, ensuring that player progress, settings, and preferences are retained between sessions.
PersistentDataPath:

- The Application.persistentDataPath provides a reliable, writable location for saved data on all platforms, allowing data to remain accessible across sessions.

Saving Data at Key Points:

- Save data automatically at key points, like level completion, character upgrades, or before quitting. This enhances the player experience by minimizing progress loss.

Autosave and Manual Save Options:

- Consider implementing both autosave and manual save options. Autosave can periodically save player data, while manual save allows players to control their progress.

Creating a save system in Unity involves understanding serialization, file I/O, and data persistence best practices. Using JSON or binary serialization allows for flexible, structured data storage, while implementing multiple save slots provides players with a richer experience. By mastering these techniques, you can create a robust save and load system, ensuring that players retain their progress and preferences across game sessions.

Building a Complete Game Project

B uilding a full game project requires a clear vision, structured planning, and an understanding of design and scope. This chapter covers the essential steps in planning a game, from defining objectives and core mechanics to creating a Game Design Document (GDD) that organizes ideas and keeps development on track. Proper planning ensures that your game project remains manageable, on schedule, and consistent with your initial goals.

Planning Your Game: Design and Scope

The design and scope of a game define its overall complexity, style, and structure. Knowing your game's intended scale, audience, and gameplay style helps you make informed decisions throughout the development process.

1. Determining Game Scope and Constraints
Identify the Project's Scope:

- Scope refers to the overall scale and ambition of the project, including the number of levels, complexity of mechanics, and amount of content.
- Determine whether you're building a small-scale arcade game, a mid-sized platformer, or a complex RPG. Keep scope aligned with available resources to avoid burnout and missed deadlines.

Setting Realistic Constraints:

- Recognize your limitations in terms of time, budget, and experience. Smaller teams or solo developers may need to simplify mechanics or reduce content to keep development feasible.
- Consider technical constraints, such as target platform limitations (e.g., mobile vs. PC) or graphics performance, which may impact the game's graphical fidelity, animations, and audio.

Audience and Platform:

- Identifying your target audience helps refine the game's style, mechanics, and challenge level. Determine whether the game is aimed at casual players, enthusiasts, or a niche audience.
- Consider the primary platform, as different platforms may require distinct controls, screen resolutions, or input methods (e.g., touch for mobile or keyboard and mouse for PC).

2. Game Genre and Style
Defining Genre:

- Choose a genre that aligns with your skills and interests, such as platformer, puzzle, shooter, or RPG. Genres provide a foundation for core mechanics, objectives, and level structure.

Selecting a Visual Style:

- Decide on a visual style, such as pixel art, low-poly 3D, or realistic graphics. The visual style can impact development time, asset creation, and the overall feel of the game.
- Ensure that the art style is achievable within your resource constraints. Stylized art can often be more manageable than high-detail, realistic art.

Defining Objectives, Levels, and Core Mechanics

Well-defined objectives, structured levels, and engaging core mechanics are the pillars of successful game design. Knowing what the player must accomplish, how they'll interact with the game world, and what makes gameplay enjoyable are essential for a compelling experience.

1. Game Objectives
Primary Objective:

- The main goal drives the player's actions and motivates progression. Define a clear primary objective, such as reaching the end of a level, defeating a boss, or solving a mystery.
- Ensure the objective aligns with the genre. For example, a platformer's primary objective might involve reaching a flagpole, while a puzzle game might focus on solving sequences.

Secondary Objectives:

- Secondary objectives add depth and replayability. These could include collecting items, achieving a high score, or completing challenges within a time limit.
- Secondary goals can enhance player engagement and provide optional tasks for more dedicated players without overwhelming casual players.

Win and Fail Conditions:

- Define how players achieve victory (e.g., finishing the final level or defeating a boss) and what leads to failure (e.g., losing all health or time running out). Clear win and fail conditions provide structure and direction for gameplay.

2. Core Mechanics
Core mechanics are the fundamental actions players use to interact with the game, like jumping, shooting, or solving puzzles. These mechanics form

the game's core gameplay loop, dictating how players achieve objectives and respond to challenges.

Movement and Interaction:

- Define the player's movement abilities, such as running, jumping, climbing, or flying. Movement is often the foundation of core mechanics, especially in genres like platformers or adventure games.
- Determine interaction methods, such as picking up items, solving puzzles, or combat. Keep these interactions consistent to ensure intuitive gameplay.

Challenges and Obstacles:

- Identify the obstacles or challenges the player will face, like enemies, puzzles, traps, or environmental hazards. Challenges should complement the core mechanics and reinforce the game's objectives.
- Consider difficulty progression by making initial challenges easy to introduce mechanics, then gradually increasing complexity as players become more skilled.

Reward System:

- Rewards provide incentives for player progress, such as points, power-ups, or access to new levels. Integrate rewards to reinforce objectives and encourage engagement.

3. Level Design

Levels are the stages or environments where gameplay takes place. A well-designed level guides the player through objectives, introduces challenges, and reinforces core mechanics.

Level Structure and Flow:

- Plan levels to progress in difficulty and complexity, balancing between

challenge and accessibility. Early levels should introduce basic mechanics, while later levels add more obstacles or require advanced skills.
- Use checkpoints in long or challenging levels to reduce frustration and maintain player momentum.

Environmental Storytelling:

- Environments can convey story elements through design. For example, an ancient ruin may imply a long-lost civilization, or a deserted lab might hint at a scientific experiment gone wrong.
- Add visual details and environmental clues to enhance immersion without direct narrative exposition.

Creating a Game Design Document

A Game Design Document (GDD) is a comprehensive document that outlines all aspects of a game, from concept to mechanics, visuals, and level details. The GDD serves as a roadmap for development, ensuring consistency and guiding decision-making.

1. Purpose and Structure of a GDD
Purpose:

- The GDD keeps all design ideas and decisions organized in one place, helping developers stay on track and providing a reference throughout development. It also communicates the game's vision to team members or collaborators.

Structure:

- While there's no universal format for a GDD, most include sections for game overview, objectives, mechanics, story, visual style, levels, and UI. Adapt the document structure based on the project's complexity.

2. Key Sections in a GDD

A well-structured GDD includes several critical sections:

Game Overview:

- **Concept**: A brief description of the game idea, including the genre, setting, and unique selling points.
- **Core Gameplay**: A concise overview of how players interact with the game, the main objectives, and the primary gameplay loop.

Game Objectives:

- Detail the primary and secondary objectives. This section should include how players progress through the game, win and fail conditions, and any specific challenges.

Mechanics:

- **Core Mechanics**: Detailed descriptions of the main actions players will use, like movement, combat, or puzzle-solving.
- **Supplementary Mechanics**: Additional features that complement the core mechanics, such as item collection, power-ups, or special abilities.
- **Control Scheme**: An outline of how players control the game, including key mappings or touch gestures for each action.

Levels and Environments:

- Define the number and type of levels, their unique features, and how they introduce or expand on gameplay mechanics.
- Include maps or sketches showing the layout and flow of each level. Highlight where challenges, enemies, and objectives are placed.

Story and Narrative:

- For story-driven games, outline the plot, backstory, and main characters. Include narrative progression and key plot points tied to gameplay.

Visual Style:

- Specify the art style, such as pixel art, cel-shaded, or realistic 3D. Include references or concept art to illustrate the desired aesthetic.
- List design guidelines for environments, characters, and UI elements to maintain visual consistency.

Audio Design:

- Describe the music style, sound effects, and any specific audio cues. List sound requirements for interactions, ambient sounds, or character voices.

User Interface (UI):

- Detail the UI layout, including the main menu, HUD (Heads-Up Display), and any other interactive screens.
- Describe the flow between UI screens and interactions, such as navigating menus or selecting options.

3. Best Practices for Writing a GDD
Keep it Clear and Concise:

- Avoid overly detailed descriptions that may complicate development. Focus on essential information, ensuring each section communicates core ideas clearly.

Use Visual Aids:

- Include diagrams, sketches, or screenshots for complex elements like level layouts, UI designs, or character animations. Visual aids enhance clarity and make the document more engaging.

Update Regularly:

- The GDD is a living document that should be updated as the game evolves. Regular updates ensure the document reflects the current state of the project, especially when new mechanics or features are introduced.

Establish a Consistent Tone:

- If the game has a specific theme, ensure that the GDD reflects this tone. For example, a horror game's GDD might use dark, atmospheric descriptions, while a casual puzzle game could be light and playful.

Planning a complete game project involves more than just coding; it requires structured preparation, well-defined goals, and a clear design document. By understanding the game's scope, defining objectives and mechanics, and crafting a comprehensive GDD, you create a roadmap for development that guides you through each phase.

Implementing Game Mechanics and User Controls

Effective game mechanics and responsive user controls create an enjoyable and engaging experience, empowering players to interact seamlessly with the game world. Implementing mechanics such as movement, jumping, or shooting requires thoughtful design to ensure smooth functionality, while control schemes should be intuitive and match the gameplay style.

1. Implementing Core Game Mechanics

Core mechanics define how players interact with the game and achieve objectives. Implementing these mechanics involves both scripting and ensuring they align with the game's design vision.

Movement and Jumping:

- **2D Platformer**: Implement horizontal movement with controls for jumping. Unity's Rigidbody2D component enables physics-based actions.
- **3D Game**: Implement forward, backward, and side-to-side movement with Rigidbody or CharacterController for physics-based or smoother, non-physics movement.

```csharp
public class PlayerController : MonoBehaviour
{
    public float moveSpeed = 5f;
    public float jumpForce = 10f;
    private Rigidbody2D rb;
    private bool isGrounded;

    void Start()
    {
        rb = GetComponent<Rigidbody2D>();
    }

    void Update()
    {
        float moveInput = Input.GetAxis("Horizontal");
        rb.velocity = new Vector2(moveInput * moveSpeed,
        rb.velocity.y);

        if (isGrounded && Input.GetButtonDown("Jump"))
        {
            rb.AddForce(Vector2.up * jumpForce,
            ForceMode2D.Impulse);
        }
```

```
    }

    void OnCollisionEnter2D(Collision2D collision)
    {
        if (collision.gameObject.CompareTag("Ground"))
            isGrounded = true;
    }

    void OnCollisionExit2D(Collision2D collision)
    {
        if (collision.gameObject.CompareTag("Ground"))
            isGrounded = false;
    }
}
```

Combat and Shooting Mechanics:

- Implement aiming and shooting by spawning projectiles from the player's position. In a 3D game, add an Aim feature to control the shooting direction.

```csharp
public GameObject projectilePrefab;
public float projectileSpeed = 20f;

void Shoot()
{
    GameObject projectile = Instantiate(projectilePrefab,
    transform.position, transform.rotation);
    projectile.GetComponent<Rigidbody>().velocity =
    transform.forward * projectileSpeed;
}
```

2. Responsive User Controls

User controls should be responsive and intuitive, enhancing player interaction with the game.

Control Schemes:

- Define control mappings using Unity's **Input System**. Map controls to commonly used keys (e.g., WASD for movement or arrow keys) or customize controls for console or mobile platforms.
- **Mobile Controls**: Implement touch-based controls for mobile, such as swipe gestures for movement or tap-to-shoot.

Control Feedback:

- Provide feedback for control actions, such as playing animations when jumping or sounds when firing. Feedback enhances engagement and provides intuitive responses to player actions.

Integrating 2D/3D Elements, UI, and Scoring

Integrating UI with 2D or 3D elements enables players to track their progress, access game settings, and view scores. Effective UI and scoring systems ensure a user-friendly experience and enhance gameplay motivation.

1. Creating a Score and Health System

A scoring system incentivizes players to complete objectives, while a health system adds a challenge by limiting the player's survival time.

Score Tracking:

- Create a score variable and update it based on game events, like collecting items or defeating enemies.

csharp

```
public int score = 0;

public void AddScore(int points)
{
    score += points;
    UpdateScoreUI();
}
```

UI Integration:

- Use Unity's **UI Text** or **TMP_Text** to display scores on-screen. Update the text whenever the score changes.

csharp

```
public Text scoreText;

void UpdateScoreUI()
{
    scoreText.text = "Score: " + score;
}
```

Health System:

- Implement a health variable that decreases when taking damage and resets on death.

csharp

```
public int maxHealth = 100;
private int currentHealth;

void Start()
```

```
{
    currentHealth = maxHealth;
}

public void TakeDamage(int damage)
{
    currentHealth -= damage;
    if (currentHealth <= 0)
    {
        Die();
    }
}
```

Health Bar UI:

- Use an **Image** as a health bar. Scale it based on the player's health to provide real-time health feedback.

```csharp
public Image healthBar;

void UpdateHealthUI()
{
    healthBar.fillAmount = (float)currentHealth / maxHealth;
}
```

2. Combining 2D and 3D UI Elements

For 3D games, overlay a UI canvas on the screen for scores, health bars, and timers. Use **Screen Space - Overlay** to ensure UI elements remain visible regardless of player movement.

Screen Space UI for Core Stats:

- Use a **Canvas** in **Screen Space - Overlay** mode for consistent display of scores, health, and controls. This Canvas remains fixed to the screen.

World Space UI for Environmental Interaction:

- In 3D games, use **World Space** UI for elements tied to in-game objects, like NPC dialogue bubbles or objective markers. Adjust size and positioning to make it readable at various distances.

3. Implementing Sound and Visual Effects in the UI

Enhance the UI with audio and visual cues for interactions.

Adding Sound Effects:

- Play sound effects on events like score updates, health changes, or button presses. Use an **AudioSource** to manage sound playback.

Visual Animations:

- Implement animations, such as flashing health bars or bouncing score counters, to emphasize changes and engage players.

Adding Levels and Increasing Difficulty

Creating multiple levels with varying difficulty provides a structured progression and keeps gameplay challenging and engaging.

1. Level Design and Progression

Each level should introduce new challenges, gradually increasing difficulty to keep players engaged.

Introducing New Mechanics:

- Use early levels to teach basic mechanics, such as movement or jumping, then introduce new elements like enemies, obstacles, or puzzles in later levels.
- Provide visual cues and guidance in initial levels, gradually removing them as the player becomes familiar with the gameplay.

Level Layout and Structure:

- Design levels with checkpoints in long or challenging sections to prevent player frustration. Use landmarks and unique layouts to guide players and prevent them from getting lost.
- Balance levels by spacing out challenges and rewarding exploration with collectibles or power-ups.

2. Increasing Challenge and Complexity

As levels progress, increase difficulty by adding complex mechanics or restricting resources.

Enhanced Obstacles and Hazards:

- Increase the number or complexity of obstacles, such as moving platforms, traps, or timed events.
- Introduce environmental hazards like lava pits or falling rocks to challenge player navigation.

Enemy Variety and AI:

- Add different enemy types with unique behaviors or weaknesses. For instance, include faster enemies, shielded foes, or ranged attackers.
- Increase AI complexity to make enemies respond more intelligently, such as evading player attacks or coordinating in groups.

Limited Resources and Time Constraints:

- Add resource management challenges, like limited ammunition or health pickups, to force strategic play.
- Consider adding time-based objectives that require players to complete sections quickly.

3. Implementing a Difficulty Curve

A well-designed difficulty curve ensures a smooth transition between levels, preventing sudden jumps that could frustrate players.

Gradual Increase:

- Each level should feel slightly harder than the previous one, adding minor changes in mechanics or introducing new obstacles at a manageable pace.

Adaptive Difficulty (Optional):

- Implement adaptive difficulty that responds to player performance. For example, decrease enemy aggression if the player is struggling, or increase health pickups to assist during challenging levels.

Implementing game mechanics, integrating UI and scoring, and adding structured levels are essential steps in creating a polished game. By developing responsive controls, intuitive UI, and a balanced progression system, you create a cohesive gameplay experience that encourages players to explore, engage, and enjoy the game. Through careful planning and progressive difficulty, your game will offer a satisfying journey that keeps players motivated and entertained.

Polish and Optimization

Polish and optimization are crucial final steps in game development that enhance performance, reduce load times, and refine the player experience. Optimizing scripts, assets, and overall performance is essential to creating a smooth, visually appealing game that runs efficiently across different devices.

Improving Performance and Reducing Load Times

High performance and quick load times are critical for maintaining player engagement. Performance optimization includes managing memory usage, reducing CPU/GPU load, and optimizing assets, all of which contribute to faster, smoother gameplay.

1. Reducing Load Times
Scene Management:

- Split large scenes into smaller, modular parts to reduce the initial load time and dynamically load sections as needed.
- Use **Unity's Addressables System** or **Asset Bundles** to load assets asynchronously, streaming only what's necessary.

Implementing Loading Screens:

- If the game has substantial load times, use loading screens to display progress, hints, or animations to keep players engaged.
- Use **AsyncOperation** with Unity's SceneManager.LoadSceneAsync to load scenes in the background while showing progress.

```csharp
IEnumerator LoadSceneAsync(int sceneIndex)
{
    AsyncOperation operation =
    SceneManager.LoadSceneAsync(sceneIndex);
    while (!operation.isDone)
    {
        float progress = Mathf.Clamp01(operation.progress / 0.9f);
        // Update loading UI here
        yield return null;
    }
}
```

Optimizing Texture and Model Assets:

- Compress textures to reduce memory usage and loading times. Unity's **Texture Import Settings** offers various compression options, like **ETC** for mobile platforms and **DXT** for desktops.
- Optimize models by reducing polygon count and removing unnecessary vertices. Use **Level of Detail (LOD)** groups to display lower-poly versions of objects when they are far from the camera.

2. Efficient Memory Management
Object Pooling:

- Instead of instantiating and destroying objects frequently, use an **object pool** to recycle objects, especially for repeating elements like bullets or enemies.

```csharp
public class ObjectPool : MonoBehaviour
{
    public GameObject prefab;
    private Queue<GameObject> pool = new Queue<GameObject>();

    public GameObject GetObject()
    {
        if (pool.Count > 0)
        {
            GameObject obj = pool.Dequeue();
            obj.SetActive(true);
            return obj;
        }
        else
        {
            return Instantiate(prefab);
        }
    }
}
```

```
public void ReturnObject(GameObject obj)
{
    obj.SetActive(false);
    pool.Enqueue(obj);
}
}
```

Garbage Collection:

- Minimize garbage collection by avoiding frequent allocations. Use **structs** instead of classes for small, temporary objects and avoid using strings repeatedly in loops.
- Use pooling for frequently created and destroyed objects to reduce strain on memory allocation.

3. Managing Draw Calls and Batching

Draw calls significantly impact performance. Reducing the number of draw calls and optimizing rendering can substantially improve performance.
Static and Dynamic Batching:

- Enable **Static Batching** for non-moving objects to combine them into a single draw call, reducing GPU workload.
- Use **Dynamic Batching** for small, frequently used dynamic objects. Keep in mind that only small meshes are eligible for dynamic batching, so this method is limited by mesh complexity.

Use of Atlases and Combined Textures:

- Combine textures into a single **texture atlas** to minimize material switching and reduce draw calls. This technique is particularly useful for objects that share a common texture or material.
- Unity's **Sprite Atlas** tool consolidates sprites into an atlas automatically, optimizing performance for 2D games.

Tips for Optimizing Scripts and Assets in Unity

Optimizing scripts and assets helps minimize CPU/GPU usage, ensuring smoother gameplay. Script optimization focuses on reducing unnecessary calculations and enhancing code efficiency, while asset optimization deals with managing resources such as textures, models, and animations.

1. Script Optimization
Avoiding Expensive Operations in Update:

- Keep Update() functions as lightweight as possible. Avoid using complex calculations or unnecessary operations within Update() and move calculations to Start() or Awake() if they only need to happen once.

```csharp
void Update()
{
    // Minimize calls to heavy methods here
}
```

Using Coroutines for Non-Critical Updates:

- Use **coroutines** to spread out non-critical operations over time instead of running them every frame in Update().

```csharp
IEnumerator SlowUpdate()
{
    while (true)
    {
        // Perform non-critical tasks here
```

```
        yield return new WaitForSeconds(1f);
    }
}
```

Avoiding Repeated Find Operations:

- Avoid using GameObject.Find or FindObjectOfType in Update() as these
  are costly operations. Cache references during initialization to reduce
  CPU usage.

```csharp
private GameObject player;

void Start()
{
    player = GameObject.Find("Player");
}
```

Optimizing Physics Calculations:

- Reduce physics overhead by lowering the **Fixed Timestep** in Unity's
  Time settings or limiting physics calculations to specific objects.
- Use **Physics Layers** to limit collision checks only between relevant
  layers, reducing unnecessary physics calculations.

2. Asset Optimization

Texture Compression and Import Settings:

- Compress textures in the **Texture Import Settings** to reduce memory
  usage. Use mipmaps for distant textures, reducing their resolution
  dynamically based on camera distance.

- Set **Max Size** to the smallest acceptable resolution for each texture. Use different compression formats based on platform requirements, such as **ETC** for mobile and **DXT** for PC.

Level of Detail (LOD) for 3D Models:

- Use **LOD Groups** for 3D models to load high-poly models only when necessary. Unity's LOD system lets you create multiple levels of detail and display lower-resolution models based on the distance from the camera.

Optimizing Audio Files:

- Use compressed formats like **OGG** or **MP3** for audio to save memory. Reduce audio sample rate where possible, especially for background music or ambient sounds.
- Adjust the **Load Type** for each audio file: set it to **Decompress on Load** for short sounds and **Streaming** for long audio tracks to manage memory efficiently.

Reducing Animation Overhead:

- Remove unnecessary keyframes from animations and compress animation curves to reduce the memory footprint of animations.
- Use **Animator** settings to simplify state machines for characters and other animated objects. Avoid complex, nested state machines if they're not essential to gameplay.

3. Using Profiling Tools for Optimization
Unity's **Profiler** is a powerful tool for analyzing performance. The profiler provides insights into CPU, GPU, memory, and rendering usage, helping identify performance bottlenecks.

CPU and GPU Profiler:

- Monitor CPU usage to identify heavy operations in scripts, physics, or rendering. High CPU usage in certain areas may indicate poorly optimized scripts or excessive calculations.
- Check the GPU profiler to review draw calls, shaders, and textures. Use this information to reduce graphical load and adjust visual quality settings.

Memory Profiler:

- Track memory allocation to detect memory leaks and excessive memory usage. High memory usage can cause frequent garbage collection, leading to frame rate drops and stuttering.
- Analyze the allocation of textures, meshes, and audio files to optimize asset management. Large, uncompressed textures or complex models may unnecessarily increase memory load.

Rendering Profiler:

- Identify performance issues related to rendering, such as high draw call counts or complex shaders. Consider reducing the complexity of shaders and combining meshes to decrease draw calls.

Advanced Optimization Techniques

For larger or more complex projects, consider additional optimization techniques to fine-tune performance.

Occlusion Culling:

- Use **Occlusion Culling** to avoid rendering objects that are outside the camera's view. Occlusion culling can improve performance significantly in 3D environments with many static objects.

Baked Lighting:

- Use **Baked Lighting** instead of real-time lighting for static objects. This reduces the computational load of lighting and shadows on the GPU.

Using Asset Bundles for Modular Loading:

- For large games, consider using **Asset Bundles** to load assets dynamically, allowing parts of the game to load only when needed. This reduces memory usage and load times.

Scriptable Render Pipeline (SRP):

- Unity's **Universal Render Pipeline (URP)** and **High Definition Render Pipeline (HDRP)** provide more control over rendering optimization. SRP is designed to offer performance enhancements, especially for mobile and VR applications.

Optimizing performance in Unity involves both script and asset adjustments, along with effective use of tools like the Profiler to analyze and improve efficiency. By managing memory, minimizing draw calls, and optimizing assets, you can create a smooth, responsive game that provides an enjoyable experience across a variety of devices. These optimization strategies prepare your game for the final release, ensuring it runs smoothly and maintains high performance even in complex scenes.

Testing and Debugging

Thorough testing and debugging are essential for delivering a polished, bug-free game that performs well across devices. Testing involves ensuring your game's functionality, playability, and stability, while debugging addresses any issues discovered. Testing on multiple devices and resolutions is especially important for mobile or cross-platform games, as it helps guarantee a consistent player experience.

Techniques for Testing on Multiple Devices and Resolutions

Different devices have varying screen sizes, resolutions, hardware capabilities, and control methods. Testing across multiple devices and screen resolutions ensures that your game adapts effectively to each environment, providing a seamless experience regardless of hardware limitations.

1. Cross-Platform Compatibility Testing
Unity Build Settings:

- Unity allows you to build for multiple platforms, including PC, mobile, and console. Use **Build Settings** to configure platform-specific options, adjusting graphics, resolution, and input controls as needed for each platform.

Adjusting Resolution Settings:

- For adaptable UI and graphics, use Unity's **Canvas Scaler** for UI elements, set to **Scale with Screen Size**. This keeps the UI consistent across resolutions.
- Test with different aspect ratios (16:9, 4:3, 21:9) to ensure visuals and gameplay remain consistent. Unity's **Game View** offers aspect ratio presets for quick testing.

Unity Remote for Mobile Testing:

- Use **Unity Remote** to test gameplay on mobile devices in real-time. This allows you to check touch input, UI scaling, and performance directly on the target device without a full build.
- Connect your mobile device via USB, then select **Unity Remote** in the Editor's **Play Mode** to view and control the game on the mobile screen.

239 .

Device Emulators and Test Labs:

- Use emulators and test labs like **Android Virtual Device (AVD)** for Android and **iOS Simulator** for iOS to simulate various devices. Google Play and Firebase also provide access to test labs for device-specific testing.
- For high-fidelity testing, consider services like **BrowserStack** or **AWS Device Farm**, which allow testing on actual devices for realistic results.

2. Performance Testing
Profiling on Target Devices:

- Use Unity's **Profiler** to assess performance metrics like CPU, GPU, and memory usage. Run the profiler on each target platform, noting performance differences between mobile, desktop, and console environments.
- Pay attention to **FPS** (frames per second), CPU/GPU load, and memory allocation to identify any bottlenecks that may affect gameplay smoothness.

Testing Battery and Resource Usage:

- For mobile games, test battery drain, memory usage, and thermal impact. High CPU or GPU load can drain battery quickly or cause the device to overheat, impacting player satisfaction.
- Monitor battery consumption with **Device Settings** on Android or **Instruments** on iOS to assess how efficiently your game utilizes resources.

Stress Testing:

- Run scenarios with high object counts, intensive physics, or complex animations to assess the limits of your game's performance.
- Implement automated testing scenarios to simulate player interactions

at scale, ensuring stability under load.

3. Input Testing
Keyboard and Mouse vs. Touch Controls:

- Test control schemes for different input methods, like keyboard, mouse, and touch, to ensure they feel intuitive and responsive across devices.
- Implement touch controls with multi-touch capabilities on mobile and ensure they don't interfere with UI elements or gameplay.

Gamepad and Controller Support:

- For console or PC games, implement and test gamepad controls. Adjust button layouts and responsiveness for both Xbox and PlayStation controllers, as well as any platform-specific controllers (e.g., Nintendo Switch Joy-Cons).

Handling Player Feedback and Iterating
Incorporating player feedback is invaluable for refining your game's mechanics, performance, and design. Regularly seeking feedback, analyzing player data, and iterating based on insights lead to a more engaging and player-centered experience.

1. Gathering Player Feedback
Playtesting with Target Audience:

- Organize playtesting sessions with players who represent your target audience. Focus on observing how they interact with the game, noting any challenges, misunderstandings, or unexpected behaviors.
- Use playtesting feedback to adjust difficulty, pacing, and UI design, addressing any pain points or enhancing popular features.

Feedback Collection Tools:

- Use in-game feedback forms or pop-ups to capture player impressions and bug reports directly. Unity's **Analytics** service also provides insights into player behavior and can track events, retention rates, and more.
- Platforms like Google Play Console and Apple App Store include user reviews and crash logs, offering valuable post-launch feedback.

Surveys and Focus Groups:

- Conduct surveys for a broad perspective on gameplay satisfaction, difficulty, visuals, and controls. Use focused questions to capture detailed feedback on specific features or mechanics.
- For deeper insights, use focus groups to discuss aspects like narrative elements, level design, and core mechanics, gaining qualitative data from targeted discussions.

2. Analyzing Player Data
Gameplay Analytics:

- Set up gameplay analytics to monitor player behavior, such as time spent in each level, frequent in-game actions, and areas where players often get stuck or fail.
- Use tools like Unity Analytics or Firebase to visualize player progression, completion rates, and areas with high player attrition.

Heatmaps and Telemetry:

- Implement heatmaps to track player movements, popular areas, and frequent interactions within the game environment. Heatmaps highlight where players spend the most time, allowing you to adjust level design or add incentives for unexplored areas.
- Use telemetry data to monitor performance metrics during play, such as frame rate, lag spikes, or memory usage at different gameplay moments.

3. Iterative Development Based on Feedback
Prioritizing Feedback:

- Prioritize feedback based on player experience, ease of implementation, and overall impact on gameplay. Focus first on critical bugs, then address gameplay improvements and quality-of-life changes.
- Segment feedback into categories (e.g., visual, performance, gameplay) to address issues systematically.

Developing Iteration Cycles:

- Establish short iteration cycles, releasing updates incrementally and using player feedback to guide each cycle. Iterative development allows you to test adjustments rapidly and see immediate player response.
- Use **patch notes** to inform players about changes and fixes in each update, reinforcing player engagement and transparency.

A/B Testing for Design Choices:

- Use A/B testing to evaluate the impact of different design choices, such as control layouts, level designs, or UI placements. Monitor player interactions with each variation to determine which version performs better.
- Implement A/B testing with a small subset of players, analyzing engagement and satisfaction metrics to make data-driven design decisions.

Effective testing and debugging involve multiple rounds of performance assessment, player feedback, and iteration. Testing across devices and resolutions ensures a consistent experience, while gathering feedback and making iterative changes refine the gameplay and address player needs. Through rigorous testing and ongoing improvement, you can create a polished, player-focused game that maintains high standards of quality and engagement.

Publishing Your Game

Publishing a game involves preparing it for launch across different platforms, setting up build configurations, and tailoring controls and UI to platform-specific needs. Proper launch preparation includes final adjustments to build settings, ensuring compatibility across devices, and creating a smooth user experience regardless of hardware.

Preparing for Game Launch

A successful launch involves more than just finalizing the game build; it requires strategic preparation, such as optimizing for target platforms, conducting a final round of testing, and setting up essential configurations for distribution.

1. Creating a Launch Plan
Platform-Specific Requirements:

- Different platforms, such as PC, mobile, and consoles, have unique requirements for asset formats, control schemes, and performance standards. Research and document each platform's guidelines to ensure compliance.
- Plan the submission and certification process based on each platform's guidelines. For example, console games require certification from Sony, Microsoft, or Nintendo, while mobile games go through app stores like Google Play and Apple App Store.

Optimizing for Target Platforms:

- Fine-tune graphics settings to balance quality and performance for each platform. For instance, reduce texture resolution or lighting complexity for mobile devices to optimize performance.
- Configure quality settings in Unity's **Quality Settings** to create separate profiles for each platform (e.g., high settings for PC, medium for consoles, low for mobile).

Pre-Launch Testing:

- Conduct final QA testing to ensure that gameplay, performance, and UI are optimized across target devices. This includes testing screen resolution adjustments, control schemes, and performance metrics.
- Perform compatibility tests on as many devices as possible, especially if releasing on mobile, to address hardware-specific issues before launch.

2. Setting Up Marketing and Community Engagement
Marketing Assets and Launch Trailer:

- Create promotional assets like screenshots, trailers, and gameplay videos that showcase the game's unique features. Platforms like Steam, Google Play, and Apple App Store have specific requirements for image and video dimensions.
- Prepare a launch trailer that highlights core gameplay mechanics, storyline elements, and visual style. Trailers are valuable assets for social media, app stores, and platform-specific promotional events.

Community Building:

- Start building a community on social media or forums before launch to generate interest. Platforms like Twitter, Reddit, and Discord offer avenues to engage with potential players and build anticipation.

- Consider establishing early access or beta testing for community feedback, allowing players to preview the game and provide insights that can refine gameplay further.

Pricing and Monetization Strategy:

- Define your pricing or monetization model based on the platform and target audience. For mobile games, decide between free-to-play with in-app purchases, one-time purchase, or ad-based models.
- If the game includes in-app purchases, ensure compliance with each platform's guidelines on in-game transactions and implement ethical monetization strategies that avoid excessive microtransactions.

Setting Up Build Settings for Different Platforms

Unity's build settings provide options to configure your game for multiple platforms, including PC, mobile, and consoles. Configuring these settings appropriately ensures that the game performs well on each platform, adheres to platform requirements, and is optimized for the intended hardware.

1. Understanding Build Settings
Accessing Build Settings:

- Go to **File > Build Settings** in Unity to open the Build Settings window. From here, you can select the target platform, configure build options, and manage additional platform-specific settings.
- Switch between platforms by selecting the target platform (e.g., Windows, Android, iOS) and clicking **Switch Platform**. Unity may re-import assets to ensure compatibility with the new platform.

Player Settings:

- In Build Settings, click **Player Settings** to access platform-specific configurations for resolution, graphics, icon, and splash screen. Adjust these settings for each platform to ensure a seamless experience.

- Customize **Product Name**, **Company Name**, and **Version Number** in Player Settings to accurately identify and manage game versions across platforms.

2. Configuring Platform-Specific Settings
PC and Console Settings:

- For PC and consoles, set up **Resolution and Presentation** settings, such as fullscreen mode, default screen resolution, and aspect ratio. Use a default resolution that suits most monitors, such as 1920x1080.
- Configure **Graphics APIs** (DirectX, Vulkan) based on the platform requirements. DirectX is common for Windows, while Vulkan offers performance gains on platforms that support it.

Mobile Settings (iOS and Android):

- In **Resolution and Presentation**, set the **Default Orientation** (Portrait or Landscape) based on the game design. Mobile games often lock orientation to match gameplay needs.
- Adjust **Graphics APIs** for mobile, with **OpenGL ES 3.0** as the minimum, while **Vulkan** is recommended for Android devices with higher graphics capabilities.

WebGL Settings:

- For WebGL builds, ensure minimal data size by compressing assets and using **GZIP Compression** to improve load times. WebGL builds are best suited for lightweight, browser-based games.
- Disable features like shadows or high-poly models, as these can increase load times and memory usage in browser environments.

3. Customizing Quality Settings

Quality settings control visual fidelity, texture quality, and rendering complexity. Adjust these settings to create a balance between graphics and performance, which varies by platform.

Setting Quality Levels:

- Use Unity's **Quality Settings** to define quality levels such as **Low**, **Medium**, **High**, and **Ultra**. Each level can adjust properties like shadow resolution, texture quality, and anti-aliasing.
- Assign a default quality level for each platform. For example, set **High** quality on PC and consoles, but use **Medium** or **Low** for mobile devices to optimize performance.

Optimizing for Mobile:

- Disable or reduce complex lighting and shadow effects, as these are performance-intensive on mobile devices.
- Lower texture resolution and use compressed texture formats to reduce memory usage. Optimize post-processing effects (bloom, depth of field) or disable them for mobile builds.

Adjusting UI and Controls for Platform-Specific Needs

User interfaces and control schemes often require customization to accommodate the varying input methods and screen dimensions of different platforms. Tailoring these elements ensures that players have an intuitive and responsive experience, regardless of device.

1. Adapting UI for Screen Sizes and Resolutions
Responsive UI Scaling:

- Set the Canvas's **UI Scale Mode** to **Scale with Screen Size** and define a reference resolution. Unity adjusts UI elements proportionally across screen sizes, ensuring consistency in UI presentation.
- Use **Anchors** and **RectTransforms** to position UI elements dynam-

ically. Anchoring allows elements to resize and reposition correctly across devices with different aspect ratios.

Optimizing UI for Touch Devices:

- For mobile devices, design larger buttons and interface elements to improve accessibility and accuracy with touch controls.
- Ensure UI elements are spaced appropriately to avoid accidental taps. For example, provide generous padding around interactive buttons and icons.

Platform-Specific Layouts:

- Implement different UI layouts for various platforms if necessary. For instance, move essential HUD elements closer to the edges on consoles or mobile to avoid interference with gameplay.
- Use conditional code to adjust UI layouts based on platform. For example, Unity's Application.platform can detect the active platform and customize the UI accordingly.

2. Customizing Controls for Each Platform
PC and Console Controls:

- For PC, configure **keyboard and mouse** controls, ensuring that key bindings are intuitive and customizable.
- For consoles, map controls to gamepad buttons and adjust sensitivity for a responsive experience. Unity's **Input Manager** or the **Input System** can handle different control setups for each platform.

Mobile Touch Controls:

- Use **On-Screen Joysticks** for player movement and **Buttons** for actions like shooting or jumping. Unity's **UI Toolkit** or **Event System** makes it easy to implement touch-based controls.

- Implement multi-touch capabilities to enable complex gestures, such as pinch-to-zoom or swipe-to-move, if the gameplay demands it.

Game-Specific Control Adjustments:

- For games that require precision, consider adding customizable sensitivity settings for both console controllers and touch devices.
- Implement control schemes that allow players to choose their preferred method. For instance, offer a choice between virtual joystick controls and tilt controls on mobile, or allow remapping of keyboard keys on PC.

Publishing a game requires careful attention to platform-specific requirements, UI adaptability, and control schemes. Preparing for launch involves optimizing for performance, configuring build settings, and refining user interfaces to provide a seamless experience across devices. By ensuring platform compatibility and tailoring gameplay to meet the needs of different players, you lay the foundation for a successful launch and a satisfying player experience.

Exporting to PC, Mobile, and WebGL

Exporting your game to different platforms—PC, mobile, and WebGL—ensures that it reaches a broad audience. Each platform has unique export requirements and settings in Unity, so a comprehensive understanding of the export process is essential. This section will cover the specific steps and considerations for exporting and testing builds on PC, mobile devices, and WebGL.

Detailed Guide to Exporting and Testing Builds

The build process involves configuring Unity's build settings, exporting the project in the appropriate format, and testing the build on target devices. Following platform-specific guidelines and testing for compatibility helps ensure a smooth launch.

1. Exporting to PC

PC builds offer flexibility in terms of graphics, resolution, and control options. Unity supports standalone builds for both Windows and macOS, each with its own configuration requirements.

Setting Up Build Settings for PC:

- Open **File > Build Settings** and select **PC, Mac & Linux Standalone**. Choose between **Windows** and **Mac OS** from the target platform options.
- **Architecture**: For Windows, you can choose between x86 (32-bit) and x86_64 (64-bit). Most modern games use x86_64 for better performance and memory handling. For macOS, select **Intel 64-bit** or **Universal** if you want compatibility with Apple Silicon.

Player Settings for PC:

- In **Player Settings** under **Resolution and Presentation**, set the **Default Screen Width** and **Height**. Unity also provides options for **Fullscreen Mode** (Fullscreen Window, Maximized Window, Windowed), which affects how the game displays on startup.
- Configure **Graphics API** settings. Windows typically defaults to **Direct3D**, while macOS uses **Metal** or **OpenGL**. You can adjust these options depending on hardware compatibility and performance requirements.

Testing the Build on PC:

- Create the build by selecting **Build** in the Build Settings window, choosing a destination folder, and letting Unity compile the executable.

251

- After building, test on multiple monitors with different resolutions to ensure the game scales correctly.
- Test both with and without a game controller (if supported) to confirm smooth input handling.

2. Exporting to Mobile (Android and iOS)

Mobile builds require specific configurations to account for touch input, screen resolution, and limited hardware capabilities. Unity supports direct export to both Android and iOS, each with platform-specific requirements.

Android Build Setup:

- In **Build Settings**, select **Android** and click **Switch Platform**.
- **Player Settings** for Android:
- **Resolution and Presentation**: Choose the **Default Orientation** (Portrait or Landscape) based on your gameplay requirements. Set **Target API Level** to the latest available to ensure compatibility with modern devices.
- **Other Settings**: Set up **Package Name** (usually com.CompanyNam e.GameName) and configure the **Minimum API Level** based on the range of devices you wish to support.
- **Graphics API**: Use **OpenGL ES 3.0** or **Vulkan** for better performance on Android devices, with Vulkan offering improved graphics for newer hardware.

iOS Build Setup:

- In **Build Settings**, select **iOS** and switch platforms. Ensure you have Xcode installed, as iOS builds require compiling in Xcode.
- **Player Settings for iOS**:
- **Resolution and Presentation**: Choose the orientation, such as Landscape Left or Right. Apple requires a specific icon setup, so add App Icons in the **Icons** tab within Player Settings.
- **Other Settings**: Set **Bundle Identifier** (com.CompanyName.GameNa

me) and configure **Minimum OS Version** to target newer iOS versions or support older devices as needed.

- **Graphics API**: Use **Metal** as it's optimized for Apple devices.

Testing the Build on Mobile Devices:

- For Android, export the APK or AAB file by clicking **Build** in Build Settings. Test the APK on a range of Android devices with varying hardware specs.
- For iOS, build and export to **Xcode**. From Xcode, test on iOS devices by running the build on your connected device.
- Test touch controls, screen orientation, and performance under different lighting conditions, as mobile screens often vary significantly in brightness and color reproduction.

3. Exporting to WebGL

WebGL allows your game to run directly in web browsers, making it accessible without downloads. This platform, however, comes with its own limitations, such as limited memory and graphics performance, especially on older or less powerful devices.

WebGL Build Setup:

- In **Build Settings**, select **WebGL** and switch platforms.
- **Player Settings for WebGL**:
- **Resolution and Presentation**: WebGL defaults to the browser's resolution. Unity provides scaling options that adapt to the browser window's size.
- **Compression Format**: Enable **GZIP** or **Brotli Compression** to minimize the file size, reducing load times. Use **Brotli** for better compression, but verify compatibility with your hosting server.
- **Other Settings**: Limit memory usage and optimize assets to keep the game lightweight, as WebGL doesn't support large files or high graphics settings effectively.

Testing the WebGL Build:

- Test the WebGL build in multiple browsers (Chrome, Firefox, Safari, and Edge) to confirm compatibility, as each browser handles WebGL differently.
- Host the WebGL build locally or on a server, and test for load times, memory usage, and stability.
- Check for responsiveness, especially if your game includes mouse or keyboard controls, to ensure smooth interactivity.

General Tips for Testing Builds
Thorough Testing Across Platforms:

- Testing across platforms ensures a consistent experience for players. Take note of platform-specific issues, such as differences in graphics performance or control input discrepancies.
- Verify the integrity of all assets and features across devices to avoid platform-specific bugs or graphical glitches.

Address Platform-Specific Bugs:

- Each platform may have unique bugs, such as UI scaling issues on mobile or slower performance on WebGL. Use Unity's Profiler to diagnose performance bottlenecks and adjust settings accordingly.

Implementing In-Game Analytics:

- Incorporate analytics to gather data on player interactions and performance metrics. Analytics help identify areas where players may face difficulties, allowing further optimization post-launch.

Continuous Integration (CI) for Automated Builds:

- Set up a CI/CD (Continuous Integration/Continuous Deployment) pipeline to automate builds and testing. CI tools like Jenkins or GitHub Actions can help maintain a consistent build process, especially for larger teams or frequent updates.

Exporting a game to multiple platforms requires careful attention to each platform's unique build requirements, testing procedures, and optimizations. By following this detailed guide, you can ensure that your game performs well and offers a smooth, engaging experience for players across PC, mobile, and WebGL platforms. With thorough testing and platform-specific adjustments, your game will be ready for a successful, accessible launch across a wide audience.

Creating Store Assets and Marketing Materials

Store assets and marketing materials play a crucial role in attracting players and driving game downloads. These materials serve as the first impression on platforms like Steam, Google Play, and Apple App Store, making it essential to craft high-quality visuals and descriptions that capture the essence of your game.

Crafting Screenshots, Descriptions, and Trailers for Stores

A cohesive set of assets, including screenshots, descriptions, and trailers, enhances your game's visibility and appeal. Each component should showcase unique aspects of your game, from core mechanics to story elements, helping potential players understand what makes your game worth their time.

1. Creating Compelling Screenshots

Screenshots provide a visual snapshot of gameplay, UI, and key features. They should be informative, high-quality, and strategically selected to highlight the game's best elements.

Selecting Key Moments:

- Choose moments that capture the essence of your game, such as intense combat scenes, scenic environments, or engaging puzzles. Highlight features like unique abilities, characters, and immersive environments that set your game apart.
- Avoid cluttered or complex visuals that may confuse viewers. Focus on clean, visually distinct moments that make a strong impact even at smaller thumbnail sizes.

Showcasing Core Mechanics:

- Use a variety of screenshots that emphasize different aspects of gameplay, such as combat, exploration, and level design. This helps players understand the core mechanics without needing a full gameplay explanation.
- Include UI elements when relevant, but ensure they are not overly distracting. UI should be functional and clean, giving a sense of the user experience without overwhelming the visuals.

Optimizing Image Quality:

- Use the highest possible resolution supported by the platform to ensure clarity. On most platforms, including Steam and mobile stores, screenshots should be at least 1920x1080 to appear crisp on all screens.
- Save images in PNG format for lossless quality. Some stores compress screenshots automatically, so start with the highest quality possible to retain clarity post-compression.

2. Writing Descriptive and Engaging Game Descriptions

Descriptions introduce players to your game's concept, mechanics, and storyline, enticing them to explore further. A well-written description should be concise yet engaging, providing essential information in an easily

digestible format.
Crafting a Strong Opening:

- Start with a hook—a sentence that captures your game's unique appeal. Highlight the main theme or feature that sets it apart, such as "Experience a haunting journey through a desolate world" or "Challenge your skills in an endless battle for survival."
- Keep the opening clear and enticing, providing enough detail to create curiosity without overwhelming potential players with excessive information.

Describing Key Gameplay Features:

- Break down core mechanics, such as combat, exploration, and puzzles, in bullet points or short paragraphs. Clearly explain what players can expect in terms of gameplay, genre, and unique systems.
- Mention any distinct features, like multiplayer modes, customization options, or skill trees. Use active language that emphasizes interactivity, e.g., "Customize your character's abilities to conquer challenging foes."

Providing a Brief Story Synopsis:

- Offer a glimpse into the game's narrative or world to add context to the gameplay. Describe the setting, main character, or central conflict, but avoid lengthy exposition.
- Focus on the elements that shape the player experience, such as "Uncover ancient secrets in a forgotten city" or "Lead a team of heroes through treacherous lands."

Including Platform-Specific Details:

- Add information that may be important to specific platforms, such as controller support for console games, mobile-friendly UI, or cross-platform play options. Make it easy for players to understand compatibility.

3. Crafting an Engaging Game Trailer

Trailers are a powerful way to communicate gameplay mechanics, visual style, and atmosphere in a short time. A well-made trailer should be visually appealing, tightly edited, and convey your game's unique appeal.

Planning the Trailer Structure:

- Begin with a quick introduction, often using a short logo animation or impactful visual to capture attention.
- Move through key gameplay moments, like exploration, combat, and any unique abilities, with each scene lasting a few seconds. A well-paced trailer should give a sense of gameplay flow without overwhelming the viewer with too much information at once.

Highlighting Core Mechanics and Features:

- Emphasize the main gameplay mechanics early on, such as combat, puzzle-solving, or character progression. Use short, action-packed clips to convey what players will experience in-game.
- Use on-screen text or voiceover sparingly to reinforce key points, like "Battle against legendary foes" or "Master the art of stealth." Text should be concise and impactful, guiding the viewer's attention without dominating the visuals.

Setting the Tone with Music and Sound Effects:

- Choose background music that aligns with the game's atmosphere, whether it's epic, suspenseful, or serene. Avoid overpowering audio and aim for a balance between music and gameplay sounds.
- Use sound effects to enhance impact, like weapon sounds in combat scenes or ambient effects in exploration moments. Syncing sound effects

with visual actions adds to the immersion.

Ending with a Call to Action:

- Close the trailer with a clear call to action, like "Available Now on Steam" or "Download on Google Play." Include relevant platform logos and release dates if applicable.
- End with a memorable image, like the game logo or a key character, to leave a lasting impression on viewers.

4. Tailoring Assets for Different Storefronts

Each platform has its own requirements for screenshots, trailers, and descriptions. Tailoring assets for each store ensures they meet technical standards and maximize appeal.

Steam Requirements:

- Steam recommends a minimum of five screenshots, including one **Header Image** (616x353 pixels) for the storefront. Use the **Community Hub** to upload additional content, like behind-the-scenes images, developer logs, or early concept art, which can foster player engagement.
- Trailers should be under 3 minutes, with a recommended resolution of 1920x1080. Ensure the trailer highlights both gameplay and narrative elements to appeal to Steam's diverse audience.

Mobile Store Requirements (Google Play and Apple App Store):

- Both stores require multiple screenshots with specific resolution requirements (e.g., 1242x2208 for iPhone and 1080x1920 for Android). Use vertical screenshots if the game is portrait-oriented.
- Trailers can be up to 30 seconds for the App Store and up to 2 minutes for Google Play. Emphasize mobile-specific features like touch controls or accelerometer usage.

Console Store Requirements:

- Console platforms like Xbox, PlayStation, and Nintendo Switch have high standards for asset quality and promotional media. Ensure that images and trailers meet their specific resolution and format guidelines.
- Console trailers often emphasize controller-based gameplay. Tailor descriptions to include controller support, multiplayer functionality, and other console-specific features.

Tips for Creating High-Quality Marketing Materials
Maintain Brand Consistency:

- Use consistent fonts, colors, and visual styles across all promotional assets, including screenshots, descriptions, and videos. Consistent branding helps your game look polished and professional.
- If your game has a unique art style, ensure that it's highlighted across all assets to reinforce the brand identity and attract players who resonate with the visual style.

Focus on Quality Over Quantity:

- While it's important to provide multiple screenshots, each one should be carefully selected for quality and impact. Avoid repeating similar images or using low-quality screenshots, as they can detract from the overall presentation.

Utilize Community Feedback:

- Early access feedback or playtest feedback can help identify which aspects of the game resonate most with players. Use this feedback to refine descriptions and choose assets that emphasize popular features or mechanics.

Creating effective store assets and marketing materials is a vital step in a successful game launch. By producing high-quality screenshots, engaging descriptions, and compelling trailers, you can attract and retain the interest of potential players across various platforms. Tailor these assets for each store's requirements, ensuring they communicate your game's value, style, and unique appeal to maximize visibility and downloads.

Launching on App Stores and Other Platforms

Launching a game on app stores like Google Play and Apple App Store involves following each platform's guidelines for submission, approval, and release. This process includes creating developer accounts, meeting platform-specific requirements, and handling post-launch maintenance and updates. Successfully launching on multiple platforms requires familiarity with each store's submission process and a strategic plan for long-term support.

Overview of Submitting Games to Google Play and App Store

Publishing a game to Google Play and Apple App Store includes configuring app settings, preparing assets, and navigating each store's review process. Each platform has distinct requirements, from app metadata to compliance with privacy and security guidelines.

1. Setting Up Developer Accounts
Google Play Developer Account:

- Register for a **Google Play Developer** account at the Google Play Console, which has a one-time registration fee. Once registered, you can publish unlimited apps under the same account.
- Set up app-specific information, including title, description, screenshots, and an APK or AAB file. The Play Console allows for pre-launch testing and app insights, which are useful for optimization.

Apple Developer Account:

- Register for an **Apple Developer** account at the Apple Developer Program, which requires an annual fee. The account provides access to the **App Store Connect** portal, where you manage app distribution.
- For iOS builds, you'll need a Mac and Xcode to compile and upload your game. Apple's strict review process prioritizes app quality, security, and adherence to guidelines.

2. Preparing Metadata and Assets for Submission
App Title and Description:

- Craft a concise and engaging app title that reflects the game's theme or genre. For example, use keywords related to gameplay or setting to make the title descriptive yet attention-grabbing.
- Write a compelling description that summarizes gameplay, core features, and unique selling points. Use bullet points to highlight key elements, such as levels, modes, or special abilities.

App Icon and Screenshots:

- Use a high-quality, eye-catching icon that represents your game's theme. The icon is often the first visual players see, so it should be memorable and visually distinct.
- Include screenshots that meet each store's resolution and size requirements. Emphasize gameplay elements like character designs, environments, and special effects to create an appealing preview.

Privacy Policy and Compliance:

- Both Google Play and Apple require apps to include a **Privacy Policy** that explains how user data is collected, stored, and used. If your game includes ads, analytics, or in-app purchases, disclose this information transparently.

- Ensure your game complies with platform guidelines regarding content, security, and advertising. For instance, avoid inappropriate or copyrighted content that may violate store policies.

3. Submitting to Google Play
Build and Test the APK/AAB:

- In Unity, select **Build Settings** and choose **Android** as the target platform. Build the APK or AAB file and test it thoroughly on multiple Android devices to ensure compatibility.
- Upload the APK or AAB file to the **Google Play Console** under the **App Releases** section, selecting the release type (internal, closed, or open testing).

Filling Out Store Listing Information:

- Complete the **Store Listing** section, which includes title, short description, full description, and visual assets.
- Configure **Content Rating** by filling out Google's rating questionnaire, which ensures your app is rated appropriately for different age groups.

Release and Monitor:

- Publish the app to the **Google Play Store** by releasing it to production or starting with a staged rollout. Staged rollouts allow you to release the app gradually, receiving feedback from a smaller audience before full launch.
- Monitor analytics and user reviews in the Play Console, addressing issues that may arise post-launch.

4. Submitting to Apple App Store
Build and Test the iOS Project in Xcode:

- In Unity, build the project for iOS and open it in Xcode. From there, set up device compatibility, app permissions, and code signing.
- Run tests on various iOS devices to ensure the game functions smoothly, as Apple's review process rigorously evaluates app quality.

App Store Connect Setup:

- Log in to **App Store Connect** and create a new app record, entering the app name, category, and primary language.
- Upload required assets, including app screenshots, app previews (if applicable), and app icon. Apple also requires an in-depth **App Privacy Details** section detailing data usage.

Submitting for Review:

- Submit the app for Apple's review process, which can take several days. Apple assesses gameplay quality, functionality, security, and compliance with App Store guidelines.
- Monitor the app's status in App Store Connect. If the app is rejected, review Apple's feedback, address any issues, and resubmit.

Maintenance and Updates Post-Launch

Post-launch maintenance is essential for retaining players, addressing bugs, and adding new content. Consistent updates show players that the game is actively supported, increasing engagement and player loyalty.

Handling Bugs and Performance Issues
Monitoring Crash Reports and Analytics:

- Use analytics tools, such as Google Play Console, Firebase, or Unity Analytics, to monitor crash reports, usage patterns, and player feedback. Identify and prioritize critical issues, such as crashes or performance drops.

- Address device-specific issues by optimizing code and reducing memory usage. Performance issues may vary between devices, especially on mobile platforms with diverse hardware specifications.

Releasing Patches and Hotfixes:

- For critical bugs, release hotfixes to address issues quickly. Both Google Play Console and App Store Connect allow you to push updates without needing to create a new app listing.
- Schedule regular patches for non-critical issues, grouping bug fixes and minor improvements to minimize disruption to players.

Adding New Content and Features
Regular Content Updates:

- Plan and release content updates that introduce new levels, characters, items, or seasonal events. Fresh content keeps players engaged and encourages them to revisit the game.
- Announce upcoming updates in-game or on social media to create anticipation and maintain community interest.

Feature Updates Based on Player Feedback:

- Use player feedback to inform new features or improvements, such as adding a requested feature or adjusting difficulty levels. Implementing player-requested changes shows that you value community input.
- Conduct surveys or polls to directly ask players about features they'd like to see, which helps ensure updates align with player expectations.

Engaging with the Player Community
Responding to Reviews and Feedback:

- Actively respond to player reviews on app stores, especially critical

265

feedback that identifies areas for improvement. Positive responses to negative reviews can show players that you care about their experience.
- Use social media, Discord servers, or forums to engage with players, answer questions, and provide support. Community engagement fosters a loyal player base and encourages word-of-mouth promotion.

Community-Driven Events and Challenges:

- Run community events or challenges, such as high-score competitions or in-game achievements, to encourage player interaction and boost engagement.
- Celebrate milestones or updates with in-game rewards, exclusive items, or content unlocks that reward loyal players.

Managing Updates and Version Control:

- Maintain organized version control to track changes, manage update schedules, and release updates seamlessly. Use version numbering to differentiate between major updates, patches, and hotfixes.
- Inform players about each update's content through patch notes, highlighting bug fixes, improvements, and new features. Clear communication builds trust and keeps players informed.

Launching a game on app stores and other platforms requires careful preparation, from submitting the game and adhering to guidelines to maintaining and updating it post-launch. By managing bugs, introducing new content, and actively engaging with the player community, you can ensure a successful launch and sustain a loyal player base over time. This approach not only maximizes player satisfaction but also enhances the game's reputation and reach across platforms.

www.ingramcontent.com/pod-product-compliance
Lightning Source LLC
La Vergne TN
LVHW022338060326
832902LV00022B/4107